Controversies and Decision Making in Difficult Economic Times

Billie Wright Dziech, *Editor*

NEW DIRECTIONS FOR COMMUNITY COLLEGES
ARTHUR M. COHEN, *Editor-in-Chief*
FLORENCE B. BRAWER, *Associate Editor*

Number 53, March 1986

Paperback sourcebooks in
The Jossey-Bass Higher Education Series

Jossey-Bass Inc., Publishers
San Francisco • London

Ministry of Education, Ontario
Information Centre, 13th Floor,
Mowat Block, Queen's Park,
Toronto, Ont. M7A 1L2

EDUCATIONAL RESOURCES INFORMATION CENTER
ERIC Clearinghouse For Junior Colleges
UNIVERSITY OF CALIFORNIA, LOS ANGELES

Billie Wright Dziech (Ed.).
Controversies and Decision Making in Difficult Economic Times.
New Directions for Community Colleges, no. 53.
Volume XIV, number 1.
San Francisco: Jossey-Bass, 1986.

New Directions for Community Colleges
Arthur M. Cohen, *Editor-in-Chief;* Florence B. Brawer, *Associate Editor*

New Directions for Community Colleges (publication number USPS 121-710) is published quarterly by Jossey-Bass Inc., Publishers, San Francisco, CA 94104, in association with the ERIC Clearinghouse for Junior Colleges. *New Directions* is numbered sequentially—please order extra copies by sequential number. The volume and issue numbers above are included for the convenience of libraries. Second class postage rates paid at San Francisco, California, and at additional mailing offices.

The material in this publication was prepared pursuant to a contract with the National Institute of Education, U.S. Department of Education. Contractors undertaking such projects under government sponsorship are encouraged to express freely their judgment in professional and technical matters. Prior to publication, the manuscript was submitted to the Center for the Study of Community Colleges for critical review and determination of professional competence. This publication has met such standards. Points of view or opinions, however, do not necessarily represent the official view or opinions of the Center for the Study of Community Colleges or the National Institute of Education.

Correspondence:
Subscriptions, single-issue orders, change of address notices, undelivered copies, and other correspondence should be sent to Subscriptions, Jossey-Bass Inc., Publishers, 433 California Street, San Francisco, California 94104.

Editorial correspondence should be sent to the Editor-in-Chief, Arthur M. Cohen, at the ERIC Clearinghouse for Junior Colleges, University of California, Los Angeles, California 90024.

Library of Congress Catalog Card Number 85-81879

International Standard Serial Number ISSN 0194-3081

International Standard Book Number ISBN 87589-707-X

Cover art by WILLI BAUM

Manufactured in the United States of America

NIE This publication was prepared with funding from the National Institute of Education, U.S. Department of Education, under contract no. 400-83-0030. The opinions expressed in the report do not necessarily reflect the positions or policies of NIE or the Department.

Ordering Information

The paperback sourcebooks listed below are published quarterly and can be ordered either by subscription or single-copy.

Subscriptions cost $40.00 per year for institutions, agencies, and libraries. Individuals can subscribe at the special rate of $30.00 per year *if payment is by personal check*. (Note that the full rate of $40.00 applies if payment is by institutional check, even if the subscription is designated for an individual.) Standing orders are accepted.

Single copies are available at $9.95 when payment accompanies order, and *all single-copy orders under $25.00 must include payment*. (California, New Jersey, New York, and Washington, D.C., residents please include appropriate sales tax.) For billed orders, cost per copy is $9.95 plus postage and handling. (Prices subject to change without notice.)

Bulk orders (ten or more copies) of any individual sourcebook are available at the following discounted prices: 10-49 copies, $8.95 each; 50-100 copies, $7.96 each; over 100 copies, *inquire*. Sales tax and postage and handling charges apply as for single copy orders.

To ensure correct and prompt delivery, all orders must give either the *name of an individual* or an *official purchase order number*. Please submit your order as follows:

Subscriptions: specify series and year subscription is to begin.
Single Copies: specify sourcebook code (such as, CC1) and first two words of title.

Mail orders for United States and Possessions, Latin America, Canada, Japan, Australia, and New Zealand to:
Jossey-Bass Inc., Publishers
433 California Street
San Francisco, California 94104

Mail orders for all other parts of the world to:
Jossey-Bass Limited
28 Banner Street
London EC1Y 8QE

New Directions for Community Colleges Series
Arthur M. Cohen, *Editor-in-Chief*
Florence B. Brawer, *Associate Editor*

CC1 *Toward a Professional Faculty*, Arthur M. Cohen
CC2 *Meeting the Financial Crisis*, John Lombardi
CC3 *Understanding Diverse Students*, Dorothy M. Knoell
CC4 *Updating Occupational Education*, Norman C. Harris

CC5	*Implementing Innovative Instruction,* Roger H. Garrison
CC6	*Coordinating State Systems,* Edmund J. Gleazer, Jr., Roger Yarrington
CC7	*From Class to Mass Learning,* William M. Birenbaum
CC8	*Humanizing Student Services,* Clyde E. Blocker
CC9	*Using Instructional Technology,* George H. Voegel
CC10	*Reforming College Governance,* Richard C. Richardson, Jr.
CC11	*Adjusting to Collective Bargaining,* Richard J. Ernst
CC12	*Merging the Humanities,* Leslie Koltai
CC13	*Changing Managerial Perspectives,* Barry Heermann
CC14	*Reaching Out Through Community Service,* Hope M. Holcomb
CC15	*Enhancing Trustee Effectiveness,* Victoria Dziuba, William Meardy
CC16	*Easing the Transition from Schooling to Work,* Harry F. Silberman, Mark B. Ginsburg
CC17	*Changing Instructional Strategies,* James O. Hammons
CC18	*Assessing Student Academic and Social Progress,* Leonard L. Baird
CC19	*Developing Staff Potential,* Terry O'Banion
CC20	*Improving Relations with the Public,* Louis W. Bender, Benjamin R. Wygal
CC21	*Implementing Community-Based Education,* Ervin L. Harlacher, James F. Gollattscheck
CC22	*Coping with Reduced Resources,* Richard L. Alfred
CC23	*Balancing State and Local Control,* Searle F. Charles
CC24	*Responding to New Missions,* Myron A. Marty
CC25	*Shaping the Curriculum,* Arthur M. Cohen
CC26	*Advancing International Education,* Maxwell C. King, Robert L. Breuder
CC27	*Serving New Populations,* Patricia Ann Walsh
CC28	*Managing in a New Era,* Robert E. Lahti
CC29	*Serving Lifelong Learners,* Barry Heermann, Cheryl Coppeck Enders, Elizabeth Wine
CC30	*Using Part-Time Faculty Effectively,* Michael H. Parsons
CC31	*Teaching the Sciences,* Florence B. Brawer
CC32	*Questioning the Community College Role,* George B. Vaughan
CC33	*Occupational Education Today,* Kathleen F. Arns
CC34	*Women in Community Colleges,* Judith S. Eaton
CC35	*Improving Decision Making,* Mantha Mehallis
CC36	*Marketing the Program,* William A. Keim, Marybelle C. Keim
CC37	*Organization Development: Change Strategies,* James Hammons
CC38	*Institutional Impacts on Campus, Community, and Business Constituencies,* Richard L. Alfred
CC39	*Improving Articulation and Transfer Relationships,* Frederick C. Kintzer
CC40	*General Education in Two-Year Colleges,* B. Lamar Johnson
CC41	*Evaluating Faculty and Staff,* Al Smith
CC42	*Advancing the Liberal Arts,* Stanley F. Turesky
CC43	*Counseling: A Crucial Function for the 1980s,* Alice S. Thurston, William A. Robbins
CC44	*Strategic Management in the Community College,* Gunder A. Myran
CC45	*Designing Programs for Community Groups,* S. V. Martorana, William E. Piland
CC46	*Emerging Roles for Community College Leaders,* Richard L. Alfred, Paul A. Elsner, R. Jan LeCroy, Nancy Armes
CC47	*Microcomputer Applications in Administration and Instruction,* Donald A. Dellow, Lawrence H. Poole

CC48 *Customized Job Training for Business and Industry,* Robert J. Kopecek, Robert G. Clarke
CC49 *Ensuring Effective Governance,* William L. Deegan, James F. Gollattscheck
CC50 *Strengthening Financial Management,* Dale F. Campbell
CC51 *Active Trusteeship for a Changing Era,* Gary Frank Petty
CC52 *Maintaining Institutional Integrity,* Donald E. Puyear, George B. Vaughan

Contents

Editors's Notes 1
Billie Wright Dziech

Part 1. Part-Time Faculty

Chapter 1. Part-Time Faculty: The Value of the Resource 7
William R. C. Munsey
The advantages of employing part-time faculty in an era of financial retrenchment are numerous and compelling.

Chapter 2. Part-Time Faculty, Full-Time Problems 15
David Hartleb, William Vilter
The short-term cost effectiveness of part-time faculty creates long-term losses.

Chapter 3. Part-Time Faculty: Nemesis or Savior? 23
George B. Vaughan
Part-time faculty are necessary to the very survival of community colleges as they exist today. Colleges must learn to assess the overall savings and costs of employing them.

Part 2. The Controversy of the Open Door

Chapter 4. The Fading Vision of the Open Door 33
Marc A. Nigliazzo
Community colleges may no longer be able to afford the idealistic vision of the open door.

Chapter 5. Keeping the Open Door Open 41
William E. Demaree
Traditional arguments against expensive open-admissions policies have lost their validity as the composition of the community college student body has changed radically in recent years.

Chapter 6. Student Enrollment: Ways to Maintain the Commitment 47
Gustavo A. Mellander
Community colleges must use increasingly limited public funds to maintain the open door, but they should also enforce rigorous academic standards.

Part 3. Retrenchment and Quality

Chapter 7. Maintaining Commitment to Quality Education 57
John M. McGuire, Eldon Miller
The commitment to quality education in the midst of declining enrollments and budgets requires community colleges to consider more than student credit hours and costs per student when cutting back programs.

Chapter 8. Weak Programs: The Place to Cut 65
Ronald J. Temple
As financial woes for colleges mount, there is a clear and persuasive argument for selective program elimination to counter economic deficiencies.

Chapter 9. Preserving and Enhancing Quality Through Effective 71
Program Evaluation
Al Smith
Decisions as to whether or not educational programs should be dropped or cut back should be based on data gathered from an effective program evaluation system.

Part 4. Differential Salaries for Faculty

Chapter 10. If You're So Smart, Why Aren't You Rich? 81
Phyllis Woloshin
Salary disparities are antithetical to the realities and values of community colleges.

Chapter 11. Competing with the Marketplace: The Need to Pay Some 87
Faculty More
Thomas E. Wagner
The principle of pay for top market value is not a theory but a necessity, and it can work effectively if the institution and its personnel are willing to recognize individual circumstances and to work together to develop a more coherent salary policy.

Chapter 12. New Approaches to Faculty Compensation 93
James L. Wattenbarger
Economic pressures have resulted in institutions' paying some faculty more than others. Many are concerned about the growing gap in pay between humanists and social scientists, as opposed to faculty with high open-market value.

Part 5. Further Sources of Information

Chapter 13. Sources and Information: Decision Making in Hard 101
Economic Times
Jim Palmer
This chapter provides further sources of information on controversial issues facing community college decision makers.

Index 113

Editor's Notes

I've often wondered if T. S. Eliot had community colleges in mind when he observed, "Humankind cannot bear much reality." The realities we face at the end of the twentieth century may not be unbearable, but they are painful and enigmatic. Community colleges were conceived from all that is best in educators. Long before it became popular to do so, we had looked at undergraduate education and found it wanting. It did not meet the needs of the majority of people, and so we reached out to the academically and economically disadvantaged, to older and working students, to all those with whom baccalaureate institutions could not or would not cope. In order to do so, we had to reaffirm our commitment to teaching, a responsibility that had lost priority in many four-year institutions. And while we struggled long—and frequently unsuccessfully—over curricular issues, we did so as equals, with little awareness that we might eventually be pitted against one another in disputes over salary differentials, part-time employment, and even the very missions of our institutions.

What makes reality so hard to bear is that it changes more rapidly than we. In the beginning, community colleges had too few students, too few faculty, too little money. Then, before we were ready, there were faculty and student surpluses; buoyed by prosperity that seemed endless, we constructed facilities and initiated programs that were not always designed for future contingencies. When the future arrived in the form of recession, some of us were very nearly impotent in the face of adversity. We had not recovered from the severity of that recession when we were confronted with government budget cuts for which not even reduced inflation could compensate.

And what of tomorrow? Can we predict the future? And if we can, will we be any wiser in dealing with its realities? The one certainty from which there is no escape is that troubled economic times are here to stay—at least for the foreseeable future. We can expect not more but less help from every level of government, especially the federal. Worse still, many of our institutions are confronting serious enrollment declines that will significantly reduce tuition income. Meyer (1985, p. 3) points out that two-year colleges are suffering their largest enrollment declines in more than twenty years. The shrinking pool of potential student constituencies may have long-term financial effects on many of our institutions. Even tuition increases cannot solve the conomic plight of higher education, because it is a labor-intense industry with very limited financial flexibility. Low faculty pay poses a serious threat to most institutions where faculty purchasing power is well below its 1970-71 level. A recent AAUP survey ("Starting the Upward Climb," 1985, p. 7) contends that an 18.9 percent increase would be necessary to reach that level. The consequence is an "alienated and isolated" professoriate (Evangelauf, 1985, p. 1) rapidly forsaking the profession.

Are we then without hope? Has reality finally become too much to bear? I think not. In reading the following articles, one can detect the same mixture of idealism and pragmatism that brought community colleges into being. William E. Demaree (Chapter Five) tells us that the most central of our missions has not and cannot be forsaken; John M. McGuire and Eldon Miller (Chapter Seven), that quality education remains our central commitment, however threatening our economic dilemmas. Phyllis Woloshin (Chapter Ten) reminds us that in a confusing world of market-driven salaries, we must hold to our belief in the education of the whole human being. Marc A. Nigliazzo (Chapter Four), Thomas E. Wagner and Ronald J. Temple (Chapters Eleven and Eight) are the pragmatists who make us realize, as pragmatists do, that ideals are costly and must at times be tempered. David Hartleb and William Vilter (Chapter Two) debate with William R. C. Munsey (Chapter One) the pros and cons of part-time faculty, who create both obstacles and opportunities for the community college.

But, however enthusiastic their arguments, none of these authors denies the validity of the others' basic concerns. It is in their recognition of shared goals and shared sacrificing of ideals that our hope lies. The debates are not acrimonious. They are pained expressions of the realities with which we, in different ways, are attempting to cope. Gustavo A. Mellander (Chapter Six), Al Smith (Chapter Nine), George B. Vaughan (Chapter Three), and James L. Wattenbarger (Chapter Twelve) remind us that we can survive financial adversity, that with courage and creativity we can discover solutions to even the most difficult problems.

This is, after all, what community colleges have always done best— searched for practical ways to alter adversities. Unlike institutions grown complacent because of huge research grants and alumni endowments, community colleges have had to struggle from their inceptions. One of the advantages is that along the way many acquired what Hemingway might call "grace under pressure." Reality, even in its starkest forms, cannot defeat us, because we have seen it all and survived it all before. Financial adversity is no stranger to the community college, and coping with the realities it imposes upon us is not an unsupportable burden.

Billie Wright Dziech
Editor

References

Evangelauf, J. "Colleges Must Hire 500,000 Professors in the Next 25 Years, New Study Finds." *Chronicle of Higher Education*, November 7, 1985, pp. 1, 29.
Meyer, T. J. "Two-Year Colleges Facing Serious Enrollment Decline." *Chronicle of Higher Education*, November 7, 1985, p. 3.
"Starting the Upward Climb." *Academe*, 1985, *71* (2), 3-74.

Billie Wright Dziech is professor of language arts and acting assistant to the dean at the University of Cincinnati's University College.

Part 1. Part-Time Faculty

*The advantages of employing part-time faculty in an era of
financial retrenchment are numerous and compelling.*

Part-Time Faculty: The Value of the Resource

William R. C. Munsey

The advantages that community colleges gain from hiring part-time faculty are of particular importance at the present time, when institutions face budget retrenchment at state and federal levels and difficulties predicting with accuracy future enrollment patterns. Even apart from these factors, there are numerous and substantial benefits that can accrue to community colleges as a result of using part-time faculty members.

Employment of part-time faculty by two-year colleges is not a new phenomenon. As early as 1931, Eells, in his classic work on the junior college, gave a list of ways how and reasons why two-year schools might find it advantageous to use part-time faculty. These included drawing on the expertise of members of the community with special skills; using full-time faculty from nearby universities on a part-time basis; employing local high school teachers who could offer continuity between high school and junior college programs, and who thus could provide better teaching than might otherwise be available; and establishing considerable variety in the curriculum (p. 396).

The most substantial growth in part-time faculty at community colleges, however, has occurred within the past ten to fifteen years. In 1971-72, 40 percent of all community college faculty were considered to be part-time. By 1981, the figure had grown to 57 percent (Bender and Hammons, 1972; Hammons, 1981). Some schools had considerably higher proportions; in 1984, for example, approximately 72 percent of all faculty members at Piedmont Virginia Community College were classified as part-time (Perkins, 1984). These part-time teachers taught approximately 50 percent of the courses at the college.

Financial Considerations

There are a number of distinct and important advantages that the use of part-time faculty affords to American community colleges in the 1980s. The most prominent of these advantages is financial. A typical class taught by a part-time teacher costs at most only 50 to 80 percent as much as the same class taught by a full-time teacher (Lombardi, 1976), and there is evidence that the use of part-time rather than full-time faculty does not reduce the quality of education received by the students (Cruise, Furst, and Klimes, 1980; Lolley, 1980; Willett, 1980). Yet this class generates the same amount of state funding per enrolled student as it would if it were taught by a full-time instructor (Guthrie-Morris, 1979). It is no wonder that the latter author comments, "It has been suggested that part-time faculty have been the moneymakers for community colleges" (Guthrie-Morse, 1979, p. 15). These considerable savings are realized because part-time faculty are paid at considerably lower rates per credit hour than are full-time faculty and because these part-time faculty members are given few fringe benefits, such as health and retirement insurance and office space.

An estimate of the cost effectiveness of part-time faculty can be made on the basis of Yarborough's (1982) cost-effectiveness formula. If all factors other than salary in this formula are held constant, we obtain the following results. A typical beginning salary for a full-time faculty member with a master's degree is around $18,000. Typical course loads for full-time faculty are twelve to fifteen credit hours per quarter, or thirty-six to forty-five credit hours per year, excluding the summer session. Division of salary by total hours taught yields amount of salary per credit hour taught, excluding fringe benefits. Using the above figures for salary and hours taught, we obtain $500 per credit hour (for a load of thirty-six hours per year) and $400 per credit hour (for a load of forty-five hours per year).

If we consider $220 per credit hour (the current pay rate for the majority of part-time faculty at Piedmont Virginia Community College) as representative of part-time faculty pay, we can obtain quantitative estimates of the cost of a course taught by a part-time faculty member, as compared to the cost of one taught by a full-time faculty member. We divide the part-time pay rate by the full-time pay rate and multiply the result by 100 percent. The cost effectiveness of employing part-time faculty is then obtained by calculating the inverse of the cost ratio per credit hour:

Part-time credit Hours taught	Full-time pay Per credit hour	Cost ratio per credit hour (part-time/full-time)	Cost Effectiveness
36	$500	44%	2.27
45	$400	55%	1.82

Fringe benefits paid to full-time faculty members, if included in the calculations, would increase the cost effectiveness of part-time teachers; nonteaching services, which part-time instructors normally do not perform, would decrease the cost effectiveness. These data provide a rough quantitative illustration, which shows an even more significant financial advantage than does Lombardi's (1976) estimate, of the cost effectiveness of part-time faculty. It should be noted that the efficiencies shown above, since they are calculated on a per-credit-hour basis, are independent of the number of credit hours taught by part-time faculty members.

At least two inferences concerning part-time faculty and class size can be drawn from these cost effectiveness data. The first is that a class with a constant number of students will cost a community college less to offer if the class is taught by a part-time instructor than if it is taught by a full-time instructor (assuming, of course, that use of the part-time instructor does not decrease the teaching load of a full-time instructor who is already on the faculty). The second inference is that, given the same assumption, employing part-time faculty enables a college to have a smaller student-faculty ratio without a decrease in overall cost effectiveness. If we assume a relatively low cost-effectiveness advantage of 1.8 for part-time faculty, then a class of ten students taught by a part-time faculty member will cost the same as a class of eighteen students taught by a full-time instructor.

Increasing the Scope of Course Offerings

A second advantage of part-time faculty is related to the assertion by Eells (1931) that their use would allow schools to offer a variety of courses. In an era of economic uncertainty, part-time faculty give the college considerable flexibility in the curriculum, without excessive cost. By employing part-time faculty, a community college can offer courses in academic areas in which enrollment is not sufficiently large to justify the hiring of a full-time instructor (Lombardi, 1975, p. 2; Cohen and Brawer, 1982, p. 70). Seasonal courses, such as gardening, dendrology, tennis, and skiing, can be offered by part-time instrucors who would teach only during the seasons of their specialties. Experiental courses, such as minicourses during the winter break or at the end of the spring term, can be offered by part-time instructors as a means of trying out new timing arrangements for courses, without placing additional, temporary burdens on full-time instructors.

In addition, part-time faculty can be employed to teach classes at off-campus locations and during odd time slots, such as evenings and Saturdays (Hammons, 1981). These time slots and locations, which may not be particularly attractive to full-time faculty members, may be ideally suited to individuals who work at other, full-time jobs during the day but wish to share their expertise in teaching roles on evenings or Saturday mornings, or may suit the well-educated homemaker or retired person who does not wish to work full-time but who desires a part-time position that provides opportunities for the sharing of knowledge and skills. The advantage to students of having classes available during evenings and Saturdays is obvious and considerable. A student who holds a daytime job will, in many cases, simply not be able to obtain release time to take a day course at a university; if the course is offered at night, the student will be able to take it without having to obtain release time. The summer short course, which can be designed to appeal to teachers or to four-year college students on summer vacation, as well as to the community in general, is another type of course suited to the part-time faculty member. Due to its brief nature and its unpredictable enrollment, the brief summer course can be offered by a part-time instructor, perhaps a full-time teacher at another college or a high school teacher, who might be unavailable during the regular school session. If such minicourses become permanent curricular fixtures, continued use of part-time faculty members in these positions will keep full-time instructors from having to assume heavy responsibilities for intense, brief courses in the middle—or at the end—of quarters.

Another advantage of part-time faculty in an era of financial retrenchment is that they can provide highly specialized expertise for limited expenditure. Dentists, lawyers, computer experts, ministers, and other professionals from the community teach courses in their areas of specialization; in so doing, they are able not only to impart their skills to others but also to obtain some of the unseen fringe benefits of teaching—providing service to the community, reviewing the basics of their own professions, and increasing their proficiency in articulating their professional expertise. Students, too, are in a position to benefit from receiving instruction from professionals other than full-time teachers. For instance, an instructor whose familiarity with real estate derives from practical office experience as well as from classroom theory has insights into the everyday workings of the profession that a full-time teacher with little or no first-hand experience outside the classroom might lack.

Other Benefits

Still another benefit of employing part-time faculty is the freedom their use gives colleges to adjust to rapid increases or decreases in enrollment. This is an enormous financial advantage. When enrollments are rising, part-time faculty, who are often readily available in the service area of a community college (Bender and Breuder, 1973; Hammons, 1981), can be hired to teach extra sections of popular courses. In times of dropping enrollment, these part-time faculty, whose contracts normally run for only one semester or one quarter at a time, can be laid off by simply not rehiring them (Price and Lane, 1976; Abel, 1977; Friedlander, 1979; Guthrie-Morse, 1979; Hammons, 1981). This flexibility is particularly useful for courses in basic skills, such as English and mathematics, which tend to have large enrollments. In the case, for instance, of a mathematics course that has twenty sections with an average enrollment of 15 students per section, for a total enrollment of 300, a ten percent drop in enrollment represents a loss of 30 students—which can be handled by the cancellation of two sections taught by part-time teachers. (A course with a smaller enrollment would not necessarily require such flexibility; a loss of 10 percent of the students from a 30-student course with two 15-student sections would be a loss of only 3 students and would probably not require the cancellation of any sections.)

Another advantage of part-time faculty at community colleges, one not often mentioned, is that the use of part-time faculty can provide an experienced pool of individuals from which a community college can select instructors for full-time positions when such positions become available. This, too, represents potential savings for the institution. According to Cooke and Hurlbut (1976) and Abel (1977), there is considerable interest among many part-time faculty in obtaining full-time appointments. A person who has been teaching on a part-time basis at a school for a number of years, who has demonstrated competence as a teacher during that time, and who is interested in a full-time position can offer to a community college experience, proved ability, and familiarity with the particular school. Less orientation would be required for such a person than would be required for someone coming into the college fresh out of graduate school or even from another teaching position, and there would be a very limited transition period, since the individual would not have to become familiar with the school or with the community it serves.

An area in which part-time faculty can be either a potential financial advantage or disadvantage to the community college is that of public relations (Bramlett and Rodriguez, 1982–83). Since a community college is specifically designed to serve the community in which it is located, and since it is safe to assume that most employees of the college, both full- and part-time, live in the region served by the college, every employee is a potential public relations person for—or against—the college. This is particularly likely to be true of a college's part-time faculty, most of whom hold full-time professional positions within the community in addition to their part-time positions at the college.

Part-time faculty members who are satisfied with their positions and who actually feel like part of the college will represent the college well in the workplace and in the community. A fairly substantial number of individuals in a college's service area will, at one time or another, be interested in taking courses at the community college for reasons of personal or professional interest. Because part-time faculty members are generally visible in their communities, and because the profession of college teaching is one that tends to command respect from the public, individuals interested in taking community college courses are likely to make this interest known to part-time teachers with whom they have contact and to ask these part-time teachers for advice or information about courses and curricula. Such occasions tend to reveal a part-time teacher's opinion of the college. An individual who enjoys teaching at the college and who believes in what the college is doing will be likely to respond with encouragement and enthusiasm. In contrast, a part-time teacher who has, for whatever reasons, become disenchanted with the college is likely to convey this disenchantment when responding to such inquiries. The satisfied teacher will have a positive effect for the college within the community; students will be encouraged to enroll because of his attitude, and the college's image and FTEs will benefit. The effect of the dissatisfied teacher will, of course, be precisely the opposite.

The morale of part-time faculty will not only affect student enrollments and community attitudes; it will also affect, for better or for worse, future recruitment of additional part-time faculty members. If a college's part-time faculty find the college to be a good place to teach, additional qualified individuals from the community will be encouraged to apply for available part-time teaching positions; as a result, the college will benefit from the larger pool of qualified potential part-time teachers. In contrast, the disenchantment of part-time teachers who find teaching at the college to be a negative experience will be likely to discourage others from consideration of part-time teaching positions at the college, and the college will be less likely to attract qualified teachers.

In summary, the very nature of the community college and of its relationship to the community creates a situation that makes the employment of part-time faculty highly advantageous. Economically, the community college can benefit substantially by the use of part-time teachers, a factor of increasing importance in this era of fluctuating enrollments and of wholesale governmental budget cutting. In terms of its ability to serve the community, the college is able to offer a greater variety of courses at a greater variety of hours and locations than it could readily provide by using full-time faculty alone. Sections of courses can be added or cancelled, as necessary, without jeopardizing the positions of full-time faculty members. Courses can be taught by individuals with hands-on expertise in their fields, as well as by career teachers, providing at great savings new perspectives to students in professional fields. Part-time faculty, many of whom would be interested in full-time positions if such positions were available, can provide a pool of experienced instructors from which full-time personnel can be hired as needed. Finally, part-time teachers can serve as a source of public relations for the college, since most part-time teachers also hold full-time positions in the community. When treated with proper respect and consideration by the college, they can serve as sources of encouragement both to prospective students and to other potential part-time teachers, strengthening the image of the college in the community.

References

Abel, E. K. "Invisible and Indispensable: Part-Time Teachers in California Community Colleges." *Community/Junior College Research Quarterly*, 1977, *2* (1), 77–91.
Bender, L. W., and Breuder, R. "Part-Time Teachers—'Step-Children' of the Community College." *Community College Review*, 1973, *1* (1), 29–37.
Bender, L. W., and Hammons, J. O. "Adjunct Faculty: Forgotten and Neglected." *Community and Junior College Journal*, 1972, *43* (2), 20–24.

Bramlett, P., and Rodriguez, R. C. "Part-Time Faculty: Full-time Concern." *Community and Junior College Journal*, 1982-83, *53* (4), 40-43.

Cohen, A. M., and Brawer, F. B. *The American Community College*. San Francisco: Jossey-Bass, 1982.

Cooke, H. L., and Hurlbut, A. S. "Part-Time Faculty Needs Full-Time Support." *Community College Review*, 1976, *4* (1), 15-18.

Cruise, R. J., Furst, L. G., and Klimes, R. M. "A Comparison of Full-Time and Part-Time Instructors at a Midwestern Community College." *Community College Review*, 1980, *8* (1), 52-56.

Eells, W. C. *The Junior College*. Boston: Houghton Mifflin, 1931.

Friedlander, J. "An ERIC Review: Instructional Practices of Part-Time and Full-Time Faculty." *Community College Review*, 1979, *6* (3), 65-72.

Guthrie-Morse, B. "The Utilization of Part-Time Faculty." *Community College Frontiers*, 1979, *7* (3), 8-17.

Hammons, J. O. "Adjunct Faculty: Another Look." *Community College Frontiers*, 1981, *9* (2), 46-53.

Lolley, J. L. "A Comparison of the Use of Instructional Resources by Full-Time and Part-Time Teachers." *Community/Junior College Research Quarterly*, 1980, *5* (1), 47-51.

Lombardi, J. *Part-Time Faculty in Community Colleges*. Topical Paper No. 54. Los Angeles: ERIC Clearinghouse for Junior Colleges, 1975. (ED 115 316)

Lombardi, J. "Salaries for Part-Time Faculty: New Trends." *Community College Review*, 1976, *3* (3), 77-88.

Perkins, J. R. *PVCC Report to the Southern Association of Colleges and Schools*. Charlottesville: Piedmont Virginia Community College, 1984.

Price, P. H., and Lane, W. H. "An Analysis of Community and Junior College Use of Part-Time Faculty." Unpublished paper, 1976. (ED 121 362)

Willett, L. H. "Comparison of Instructional Effectiveness of Full- and Part-Time Faculty." *Community/Junior College Research Quarterly*, 1980, *5* (1), 23-30.

Yarborough, N. P. "Taking a Look at Cost Effectiveness Via Faculty Loads." *Community and Junior College Journal*, 1982, *82* (5), 21-24.

William R. C. Munsey is lecturer in chemistry at Piedmont Virginia Community College in Charlottesville.

The short-term cost effectiveness of part-time faculty creates long-term losses.

Part-Time Faculty, Full-Time Problems

David Hartleb
William Vilter

In era of financial uncertainty, the appropriate use of part-time faculty in community colleges poses a number of challenging questions. What is the appropriate mix of full- and part-time faculty in a department or program? When are there too many or too few part-time faculty members, or can there be too few? Although part-time faculty provide instruction at a lower cost than full-time faculty, what are the academic and instructional costs to the institution? Is there a critical mass of full-time faculty necessary to maintain the intellectual climate necessary for a healthy and dynamic consideration of the programmatic needs of the department? If an institution has a competency-based, outcome-oriented curriculum, can faculty members simply be plugged in and out of courses like workers on a production line? What is the long-term impact of employing substantial numbers of part-time faculty?

    The answers to these questions lie first in recognition of the essential purpose of education. Even when economic concerns predominate, the essence of a college education rests not primarily in the acquisition of specific and neatly packaged skills; rather, it is in the challenge to students' cultural, intellectual, and emotional growth. These attributes of a college education, sometimes called intangibles, are the most important qualities that we can transmit to our students and add to our communities. The intellectual climate necessary to achieve this experience for students can occur only where there is a faculty of full-time educators who are dedicated to their tasks. True intellectual fervor, the quest for new knowledge, free and open inquiry, and the love of learning for its own sake can occur only in an environment in which faculty are readily accessible and dedicated to the task of guiding students. We do not wish here to impugn the dedication and expertise of part-time faculty members or the invaluable contributions they make. They are generally dedicated to their tasks, they come fully prepared, and they bring enthusiasm and expertise that may be lacking in the institution.

Nevertheless, by definition they are devoting only part of their lives to this task. They very often have other, full-time professional positions. Sometimes even worse, they are putting together a living by teaching part-time at a number of institutions and thereby stretching themselves so thin and working such long and difficult hours that they are indeed part-time at each institution. We do not expect, and we rarely find, part-time faculty members participating in curriculum discussions, engaging in student advising, or finding time to pursue the broad and general philosophical questions intrinsic to intellectual environments. They typically come to campus in order to meet very specific obligations. They do their jobs well, and then they leave. If one perceives education as an assembly line, then this is satisfactory, but it is a dangerous perception, for the excessive use of part-time faculty will eventually destroy the most central function of institutions of higher education, and it must be resisted at all costs.

Part-time faculty now represent 32 percent of the teaching force in higher education and 51 percent of the faculty in two-year colleges ("The Status of . . . ," 1981, p. 29). Since these figures represent a doubling of the general numbers over the last ten years and a fivefold increase in the two-year college figures (Tuckman and Tuckman, 1980, p. 71), part-time teaching would appear to be rather attractive work for which great numbers of applications are filed. Yet finding in print evidence describing the attractiveness of the role of the part-time faculty member is difficult.

In the early 1970s, part-time faculty members were simply identified as being "cheap labor" in reserve ("Pedagogical Moonlighters . . . ," 1971, p. 12) and as "step-children" (Bender and Breuder, 1973, p. 29), but soon Blank and Greenberg (1977, 1982) identified such teaching as drudge work, which is akin to that of the migrant worker. Spoffard (1979) and McQuade (1981) continued the use of this metaphor. Part-time faculty have also been identified as "absentee faculty" (Pollock and Breuder, 1982, p. 59), a term that clearly identifies them with the host of ills associated with their landlord counterparts; as coolie labor oblivious to the "politics of the rickshaw" (Chell, 1982, p. 35); and, more gently, as the casual labor or "field hands of academe" (Spoffard, 1979, p. 14). Certainly, these are rather unattractive titles for a job classification that currently has at least 215,000 people in its ranks.

Such metaphors, penned for the most part by part-time faculty to describe themselves and by full-time colleagues to make known their concern for having participated in the creation of so many part-time positions, indicate a general unhappiness with the academic environment into which many part-timers enter. It is a complex environment of too many students and too few dollars with which to educate them well, of overworked and underpaid faculty, and of revenue-conscious legislatures interested more in capital-improvement budgets than in the quality of education within their states.

Who Recognizes the Problems?

Many academics do not see the problems created by employing large numbers of part-time instructors. One such group is that of part-timers who do not depend for their livelihoods on the academic world. They are identified in the literature as half-mooners, full-mooners, or retirees, who enjoy being asked to offer instruction in their special-interest areas, such as real estate, law, accounting, or journalism. The community college usually provides exactly what these employees want: teaching schedules that match their other commitments and the opportunity to drop into or out of teaching as their lives change. For these faculty members, the salary scales and institutional commitment are either of secondary importance or are completely unimportant. They are the few ambassadors of goodwill about whom Hammons (1981) spoke with such favor when he was a dean. Another group indifferent to the difficulties part-timers may create is full-time faculty who prefer that someone else teach the undesirable courses—those with large enrollments, remedial students, or undesirable hours.

Administrators can become shortsighted and see only the short-term benefits of employing part-time faculty. When budgets are tight, the use of part-time faculty appears to provide the flexibility that is administratively desirable. Dismissing a part-time faculty member seems easier than releasing someone in a tenure-track position. It is also easy to increase class size with a part-timer; as any administrator knows, there is a price to pay when he or she does this to a faculty member on the tenure track. Part-time faculty members are generally more cooperative and more willing to accept change than full-time, tenure-track faculty. Administrators who do not keep in mind the values of the institutions and the overall purpose of higher education can easily fall prey to the attractions such part-time employees offer.

What Are the Costs to the Institution?

While all of us should acknowledge the contribution of part-time faculty, we should also recall the statement by Wayne Booth (1981): "You can tell whether a college is serious about teaching its students at any level by looking closely at how many freshmen are taught by part-time faculty members who have no training and who have no stake in the future of the institution and its programs, no sense of how their work relates to anything else the college is doing, no long-range prospect of full-time or permanent appointments, and thus little reason to think that what they do matters to anyone'' (p. 36). In the past, institutional reputations and thus the reputation of faculty were often measured for prospective students in terms of the ratio between faculty and students. Booth obviously recognizes the development of a new measure—the ratio between part-time faculty and students as a means of establishing an institution's commitment to the education of those who register and pay for instruction. As colleges become more competitive for students, this new ratio may well become a significant factor in the decision making of the student.

While Booth's statement attacks effectively the generalized use of part-time faculty in higher education, there are specific situations in which part-time faculty bring to students exactly what they need: an orientation to specific types of work and their environments. At the same time, this argument does not begin to counter concerns that all of us should have with respect to our involvement in a system that has become heavily dependent on part-time faculty for the continuation of program offerings. This dependence is especially acute in departments that offer general education or service courses. Of concern to us should be the obvious devaluing, in terms of dollars, of what needs to be done to teach effectively.

Formulas that equate dollars for credit hours taught give very little indication of the work that must take place away from the classroom to produce effective college-level instruction. Tuckman and Caldwell (1979) point out, "Under the current reward system the incentives to maintain skills are limited and are related to nonmonetary incentives and/or left to the part-timers' other employers" (p. 759). In approving the creation of a "second class" of the professoriate, we may thus be encouraging piecemeal work for piecemeal pay.

One requirement for teaching well is the willingness to expend time planning, reviewing, and evaluating one's work. While most faculty members engage in these activities, part-time faculty quite often cannot or will not devote to all of them the time necessary. The last-minute appointments of part-time faculty members to teaching assignments make careful planning and review difficult. To compound the problem, part-time faculty members must of necessity move from one institution to another to secure employment. Again, review is difficult because instructional strategies that worked well in one postsecondary environment may not be all that effective in another. The composition assignment or historical research project that generated interest among baccalaureate-degree students may be well above the cognitive, skill, or interest levels of the students in the two-year college down the road. As a response to this problem, part-time faculty members usually adopt the departmental syllabus and the recommended text and opt to present mechanically the content of the course. Department heads and program directors cannot look askance at such "teaching." They approved the syllabi and quite often write or use the texts.

As with food in a steam tray, there is an institutional flavor to this form of teaching.

Part-time faculty also have difficulty establishing rigorous standards for student learning. They may lack knowledge of an institution's criteria or confuse the standards of different colleges if they are employed at more than one institution. Most general education classes taught by part-time faculty are required, scheduled in multisectioned units, and assigned on a contingency basis requiring a specified number of registrants before the first day of class. In multisectioned classes, where students are free to choose their instructors, part-time faculty members know that from term to term they are dependent for their salaries on student attitudes toward them. They also know that grades, high or low, are attitudinal adjusters over which they have some control. In addition to this, part-time faculty members usually teach at hours that are generally unpopular both with their full-time colleagues and with their students. Part-time faculty members must, to continue employment, present themselves to the students as attractive figures in an unattractive setting. As one adjunct instructor describes the situation, "All this makes for teaching on tiptoe" (Chell, 1982, p. 38). One way to tiptoe from term to term is through conscious or unconscious modifications in standards of assessment.

Hired at the last minute and subject to release without notice, part-time faculty members have little reason or time to plot teaching strategies that will lead their students through a full year's work. Theirs must of necessity be a no-frills approach to teaching; the basics must be without much thought for the next quarter or for experimentation that might lead to greater insight on the part of students over time. The testing of new approaches to teaching or the establishing of new goals for student learning are for part-time faculty members financially suicidal activities. For them, what is done in the classroom must satisfy the students by the end of the first week and be fairly consistent with the pedagogy of the department head or program director from the first day. For these reasons, innovative teaching, which might lead a full-time colleague toward advancement in rank or to merit awards, is discouraged in the world of part-time faculty members. The "soft sell" of general education seems to work best. Quite obviously, the softer the sell, the greater the chance of decline in the quality of education.

Of course, the hiring of part-time faculty members to fill vacancies created by the departures of full-time colleagues does save money, but only a few of the individuals involved in this transition really benefit from it. Students lose because their contact with part-time faculty members is usually limited to the hours that the classes are in session; part-time faculty members, paid per credit hour of instruction, have little incentive for remaining current in their fields or for making out-of-class time available to their students.

The departments dependent on part-time faculty to reduce the cost of instruction also lose because part-time employees are not active in departmental governance, nor are they prone to seek involvement in such activities as curriculum development or student advising. They are paid to instruct, not to participate. Thus, additional nonclassroom work must of necessity be shouldered by remaining full-time faculty. The institution may save money, but faculty lose because they are required to do more for the same amount of pay.

There may be an additional hidden cost in employing part-time faculty. Frequently, supervisors become sympathetic to part-time faculty members who depend heavily for their livelihoods on the institutions where they work. These supervisors may find it quite difficult to tell staff members that there is no teaching in the spring quarter, or to indicate that there has been a programmatic change and that their particular specialties are no longer needed. The result is that supervisors may convince themselves of, and then argue with passionate illogic for, the continuation of courses no longer necessary, because they have developed a sense of responsibility for needy part-time faculty. In some departments or program areas, friendships between full-time and part-time faculty may become stronger than budgetary considerations, and the supposed savings associated with part-time teaching are thus lost.

For some, the opportunity to teach courses on a part-time basis provides an outlet for expression or a sense of adequacy or a short-term source of income. These outcomes are important, of course, but in most cases such employment fails to provide the hiring institution or the individual hired with the opportunity of reaching the long-term societal goals that are usually associated with full-time employment at a community college. Rather, in an attempt to reduce the cost of general education courses by 50 percent or more, administrators have created a new class of instructional specialists: journeyman instructors in heavily-subscribed, multisectioned courses. Often teaching classes in several different institutions and steadfastly expressing satisfaction with their teaching roles, these individuals are still unable to do well the job that they profess to enjoy. With the doors of the guild hall closing, the journeyman instructors do the basic maintenance work of others.

What Are the Costs of Being Part-Time?

Certainly, in small communities where the local banker has taught a finance course at the community college for years, that college has an influential spokesperson. What the banker does not make in salary, he or she earns in personal development, self-esteem, and prestige in the community. In this instance, one might even accuse the banker of using the community college to further his or her nonacademic goals.

More commonly, however, part-time faculty are employed to teach large sections at undesirable times, and such personal satisfaction is not present. These faculty often are not paid on time. Once hired, they may have no access to the library or to the athletic facilities. They may well have to pay for parking and then search with their students for spaces in distant parking lots. Some must even buy their own desk copies to begin their teaching assignments. These colleagues certainly do not represent a public relations bargain for the college, because such adverse circumstances discourage them from becoming ambassadors of goodwill.

The difficulties of the part-time faculty member are compounded because it can be dangerous to become genuinely involved in departmental activity: One remark at variance with the view of a full-time colleague or committee chairperson may prejudice the hiring practices of the department for the next quarter. It is better for the part-time faculty member to remain unnoticed in the departmental office and save such argumentative comments for the other inhabitants of the part-time office at the far end of the hall. (Of course, many hiring institutions do not provide office space in which such clandestine conversations between part-time faculty could take place.)

Positions of part-time faculty members are much less secure than are those of even first-year, full-time faculty. While full-time faculty are expected to participate in discussions concerning curriculum, methodology, and textbooks, such future-oriented discussions are of little interest to part-time faculty members, who may well not be teaching in the institution during the next term.

Part-time faculty members also suffer because part-time teaching is becoming a less viable avenue for securing full-time employment at the college level. A per-credit-hour wage, with very uncertain job security, requires of part-time academicians a steady search for other income sources instead of the search for excellence in teaching, research, and service activities. Thus, when part-time faculty members, after all their years of work, usually have little to show aside from many hours of teaching, hiring institutions tend not to be responsive to arguments about FTEs of the past. The doors of the academic guild hall are shutting with increasing regularity in the faces of part-time faculty members (Tuckman and Caldwell, 1979).

Hired because their credentials meet minimum standards, because they are available at specific hours of the day, and because they will accept greater than normal student loads, part-time faculty members never make the community college their own. They are the dream of many administrators and the dilemma of most faculty collective bargainers. They do not complain. They come to campus, teach their courses, and leave for other employment or activity. They do not participate in the traditional governance system, and they rarely engage in departmental warfare. They receive no benefits, put little pressure on secretarial staffs, and certainly raise no questions as to institutional budgets or their management. But they are no bargain, not even in times of financial crisis. Until institutions are prepared to offer them more and ask less, most part-time community college faculty will mean more problems than solutions.

References

Bender, L. W., and Breuder, R. "Part-Time Teachers—'Step-Children' of the Community College." *Community College Review*, 1973, *1* (1), 29–37.

Blank, S., and Greenberg, B. "Living at the Bottom." *Writing Program Administration*, 1982, *9* (6), 9–12. (Originally published 1977.)

Booth, W. "The Treatment is Scandalous." *Writing Program Administration*, 1981, *5* (1), 35-39.

Chell, C. "Memories and Confessions of a Part-Time Lecturer." *College English*, 1982, *44* (1), 35-40.

Hammons, J. O. "Adjunct Faculty: Another Look." *Community College Frontiers*, 1981, *9* (2), 46-53.

McQuade, D. "The Case of the Migrant Workers." *Writing Program Administration*, 1981, *5* (1), 29-34.

"Pedagogial Moonlighters, The University's Cheap Labor Reserve." *Changing Education*, June 1971, pp. 12-13.

Pollock, A., and Breuder, R. L. "The Eighties and Part-Time Faculty." *Community College Review*, 1982, *9* (4), 58-62.

Spoffard, T. "The Field Hands of Academe." *Change*, 1979, *11* (8), 14-18.

"The Status of Part-Time Faculty." *Academe*, 1981, *67* (1), 29-39.

Tuckman, B., and Tuckman, H. "Part-Timers, Sex Discrimination, and Career Choice at Two-Year Institutions." *Academe*, 1980, *66*, 71-76.

Tuckman, H., and Caldwell, J. "The Reward Structure for Part-Timers in Academe." *Journal of Higher Education*, 1979, *50* (6), 745-760.

David Hartleb is acting dean at the University College, University of Cincinnati.

William Vilter is head of the Department of Language Arts in the same college.

Part-time faculty are necessary to the very survival of most community colleges as they exist today. Colleges must learn to assess the overall savings and costs of employing them.

Part-Time Faculty: Nemesis or Savior?

George B. Vaughan

The two previous chapters examined some of the issues surrounding the debate over the use of part-time faculty by community colleges, with the authors offering their observations and conclusions. One can rest assured, however, that the debate will continue, no matter how valid the points made by Munsey, Hartleb, and Vilter. The same can be said of the observations here, for the issues surrounding the use of part-time faculty, rather than subsiding, may be reaching crescendo levels as community colleges attempt to provide more services with fewer resources. In spite of, or perhaps because of, the large number of part-time faculty employed by community colleges, these individuals are still something of an unknown to much of higher education. One source (Gappa, 1984) notes that no major study has been done on the use of part-time faculty in higher education since the late 1970s and that statistics about part-time faculty are sparse and out of date. According to Gappa, "The jury remains out on the question of whether part-timers augment the quality of higher education or whether they debase it." Put another way, are part-time faculty members to be the nemesis of the community college, or its savior? Of course, on most campuses they are neither nemesis nor savior, but rather a combination of pluses and minuses that must be utilized effectively if the community college is to achieve its full potential and if it is to avoid "class warfare" among faculty members.

Arguments in favor of using part-time faculty usually center around two points, both of which bear repeating here: Part-time faculty bring greater flexibility to the curriculum and are less expensive than full-time faculty. Obviously, the two points have several facets and are often interdependent.

Arguments against the use of part-time faculty also cluster around two points: Part-time faculty detract from the collegiate nature of the institution, especially in the areas of institutional governance, committee work, and faculty interaction with students; and part-time faculty make it possible for administrators to fill virtually all new and vacant positions, thereby reducing the number of full-time faculty members and replacing them with part-timers, who tend to be more subservient to the whims of the administration. The result is that an inordinate number of part-time faculty weakens the power base of the full-time faculty. These points are also interdependent. Interestingly, the jury is also still out on the effectiveness of part-time faculty as teachers.

Part-Time Faculty: A New Perspective

Today, part-time faculty members are as prominent on most community college campuses as are part-time students. Part-timers, as they are referred to—sometimes with affection, sometimes with scorn—often teach courses that full-time faculty are either not qualified to teach or do not want to teach. They teach at night and on weekends, times that are anathema to most full-time faculty members. They work for less pay, less prestige, and less security than do full-time faculty. They are on the bottom rung of the academic ladder, a ladder most academics feel they must scale if their careers are to be successful. As Gappa observes, although part-timers are aware that full-time faculty and administrators view them as second-class citizens, part-time faculty are sufficiently satisfied to continue teaching. The obvious question is why.

A 1976 study sponsored by the American Association of University Professors resulted in a taxonomy of part-time faculty, which sheds light on why part-time faculty continue to teach. According to the study, part-time faculty fall into one of the following seven mutually exclusive categories: the semi-retired, the students, the hopeful full-timers, the full-mooners, the homeworkers, the part-mooners, and the part-unknowners (Gappa, 1984, pp. 26–28). While the seven-category taxonomy is useful in understanding why certain part-time faculty engage in teaching, it is somewhat cumbersome for this discussion. A two-category classification seems to be better suited to understanding part-time faculty who teach in the community college.

Part-time faculty members who teach in the community college can be roughly divided into two categories. The first category, which I refer to as the *independents*, are not committed to teaching as a career and are not interested in full-time teaching, unless they are already teachers at other institutions. Their livelihoods are independent of the income they receive from part-time teaching. Neither their professional nor social lives are tied closely to the college.

The second category, the *dependents*, are committed to teaching as a career and wish to pursue it full-time. They depend on part-time teaching as an important source of income. While the dependents are rarely fully accepted by the college community, they nevertheless rely on the college "family" to fulfill many of their professional needs and occasionally to fulfill their social needs. Lingering on the periphery of the academic mainstream only adds to their frustration.

Independents and Dependents: A Closer Look

The independents consist of those who teach part-time for personal reasons, such as ego satisfaction, as a means of paying their "civil rent"; or, in some cases, as a means of keeping up with the new theories and practices in their field. Falling into this category are successful lawyers (some lawyers who have failed to establish a successful practice fall into the second category); doctors; dentists; bankers; business executives; master craftsmen and technicians; upper-level managers; high school teachers; and occasionally writers, artists, politicians, actors, and others from less traditional fields. Rarely do members of this group view part-time teaching as a major source of income or as a stepping-stone to full-time faculty status, although some high school teachers may view part-time college teaching as a means of moving from secondary to higher education; indeed, it is not unheard of for some members of this group to teach for no pay or to donate their pay to the college's foundation. Members of this group normally adhere to rather rigid schedules in their full-time careers and therefore are available to teach only at certain times, usually in the evening. Members of this group tend to accept the status quo of the college, including low pay, and are not normally intimately involved in the governance process.

The dependents are individuals who are working on or who have received advanced degrees in traditional academic disciplines and who want to teach, but who are unable to find full-time positions in academic institutions. Many members of this group have new Ph.D.'s in such low-demand disciplines as the humanities and the social sciences. Married women who want to enter or re-enter the work force, and individuals who have made moves because of opportunities offered to their spouses, often fall into this category, although they may not be recent graduates. Members of this group are the itinerants of higher education, moving in and out of the college from session to session, from year to year, and in some cases moving from one college to another and occasionally teaching at more than one college during a given term. Members of this group often depend on part-time teaching as an important source of income and view part-time teaching as a stepping-stone to full-time employment. They have flexible schedules and are willing to teach anytime, anywhere, if it will advance their careers and increase their chances for full-time employment. Members of this group are likely to show up at collegewide meetings and are vitally interested in the governance process, especially as it relates to the role of part-time faculty.

The two categories are far from rigid, and the classifications do not apply to all part-time faculty, for many community colleges employ part-timers who do not fit neatly into either of the above categories. Nevertheless, the bulk of the part-timers seem to fall under the rather broad umbrellas of these two categories and will be discussed in that regard.

Two Categories, Two Approaches?

A mistake many administrators and full-time faculty make in working with part-time faculty is to assume that they are all alike. A closer look reveals why it is important to recognize the differences between the two groups while at the same time recognizing that they have much in common—they all want a desk, office space, recognition, and other amenities one normally associates with any teaching position.

The independent part-time faculty members referred to above—the doctors, practicing lawyers, and business executives—are unlikely to join any academic rebellion of part-timers, although they might join the union (hardly an act of rebellion on the community college campus today). These individuals are devoting the bulk of their time and energy to their full-time careers; teaching part-time is their avocation. One does not normally work to create undue pressure when a prime reason for engaging in an activity is to seek relief from the day-to-day pressures of one's own workday. Members of the second category are a different story, however.

The dependent part-time faculty members who are seeking full-time employment are the ones who are usually the most frustrated and the ones who want, need, and in some cases demand higher pay, job security, and a sense of belonging to a profession. Administrators simply must pay more attention to this group if open confrontation is to be avoided between part-time faculty and administrators, and sometimes between full- and part-time faculty (who have recently opposed one another on some campuses in California and other states).

Members of this group are primed to become academic revolutionaries. And why not? Most of them are highly intelligent, possess advanced degrees in their disciplines—degrees they have spent three or four often frustrating years of hard work earning. They feel cheated by the system. If not bitter, they are certainly cynical toward an institution that utilizes their talents year after year but continues to pay them paltry salaries, continues to ask them to teach courses at odd times, continues to offer them no security, and continues to view them as second-class citizens whose value to the institution is dependent on the ebb and flow of enrollments. They are potential academic revolutionaries because they are intelligent, because they are frustrated, because they are determined, and because they have little or nothing to lose by rebelling.

More rebellion does not take place because these part-time faculty members hope to obtain full-time positions with the colleges where they are teaching and because they are teachers who want to create, not destroy. Nevertheless, community college administrators may be living on borrowed time by failing to acknowledge and deal with the frustrations of this group. Joining unions is one example (although an acceptable one in several states) of a minor form of protest on the part of these faculty members.

Suggestions for Change

A number of individuals proposed improvements in dealing with part-time faculty. Parsons (1980) offers outstanding suggestions, as does McGaughey (1985), who calls for "integrity and integration" in working with adjunct instructors. Little would be gained by restating their positions here. The remainder of this chapter will be devoted to suggesting how the professional status of dependent and, to a lesser degree, independent part-time faculty can be enhanced.

None of the above-cited writings deals with the differences between independent and dependent part-time faculty, although Harris (1980) notes that from the president's perspective there is a difference. He writes:

> A community college president deals happily with the business executive, the manager, the draftsman, or the expert welder who is enriched by relaying his own expertise to students on a part-time basis. For these faculty members, teaching is an ego-renewing experience. It is also a temporary commitment secondary to a different full-time job. However, presidents deal less easily with the expectations of the graduate teaching assistant, the All But Dissertation history scholar, or the high school teacher, many of whom view their part-time employment as the first critical step toward full-time employment at the college level. *In fact, for a considerable number of these faculty members, the main source of money is part-time teaching* [pp. 14-15; italics added].

While I do not include the high school teacher in the "less easy to deal with category," and while the author fails to include the large number of "underemployed" individuals who already have the Ph.D. and who are teaching part-time, especially in community colleges that have universities in their service regions, he comes close to defining the independent and dependent part-time faculty categories I have identified. Unfortunately, from the perspective of understanding part-time faculty, he chose not to pursue the differences between the two groups, other than noting that dealing with the second group—the dependents—makes the president uneasy.

Recommendations

The following recommendations are based on the foregoing argument that there are two rather distinct categories of part-time faculty presently teaching in the community college and that the members of the two groups should be treated differently. The majority of the recommendations deal with those part-time faculty members I have described as the dependents.

1. Administrators should recognize that two categories of part-time faculty exist and that the distinguishing features of both groups are the goals of their members. One group is content to teach part-time and accepts things as they are. The other group desires to teach full-time and will work to change the system that denies this opportunity.

2. Both groups should be provided with such basics as recognition, office space, and the other essentials necessary to any teacher.

3. In recognizing the difference between the two groups, greater effort should be devoted to bringing the dependents into the mainstream of college life than is devoted to the independents. For example, the part-time faculty member with a Ph.D. in history would likely welcome the opportunity to serve on the curriculum and instruction committee, whereas the bank executive would find such service a burden. The new perspective brought to bear on collegewide issues by a new Ph.D., or by a spouse returning to the academic marketplace after a prolonged absence, can be refreshing and valuable to the institution and should not be lost simply because part-timers do not normally serve on such committees.

4. A word of caution is in order regarding the above recommendation. By involving the dependent part-time faculty in more college activities, there is some danger in raising their expectations even higher, an unacceptable state for a group of individuals who already suffer from rising expectations. Also, the line between part-time and full-time faculty will likely become even more blurred than is the case today, a situation that most full-time faculty members would find unacceptable. Nevertheless, the gamble of further involvement seems to be less dangerous than the current situation on most campuses.

5. Administrators should recognize that financial rewards are more important to the dependents than to the independents and therefore should develop a means of providing greater financial rewards for the dependents. This is easier said than done: Many colleges operate under statewide or districtwide salary scales for part-time faculty and therefore seem to have little leeway in determining part-time faculty pay. Nevertheless, part-time faculty members' work can be defined in terms of work load and not simply teaching load, a concept that most community colleges endorse but few have defined. If work load is defined in terms broader than just teaching, dependent part-time faculty can be paid for serving on committees and other activities that go beyond classroom teaching, activities the independent part-timers are not normally available to perform.

6. In line with the above, the dependent part-time faculty member can be very useful in any number of ways, such as academic advising and working with student activities, in addition to serving on collegewide committees. If part-time faculty are considered a good financial bargain today, it would seem that their value should increase as their duties increase, but they must receive additional financial rewards for these activities.

7. Colleges should adhere to strict affirmative action principles when recruiting part-time faculty. While this may appear ludicrous in "recruiting" the only real estate agent in town to teach a course in real estate, it can pay big dividends for the college and for part-time faculty who are seeking full-time employment. By utilizing sound affirmative action principles in recruiting part-time faculty, the college is not only assured of some balance among the races and between the sexes within its part-time faculty ranks but the part-timers also stand a better chance of not being eliminated by affirmative action considerations should a full-time position develop at the college.

8. By involving part-time faculty in a number of collegewide activities, by following affirmative action guidelines in employing part-time faculty, and by generally upgrading the status of part-time faculty, especially the dependents, the college will increase the value of these faculty members. This increased value and experience gained at the college should be taken into consideration if a part-time faculty member receives a full-time appointment and should result in a higher initial salary.

9. Finally, and perhaps most important, administrators and full-time faculty should exert a special effort to make the dependents feel that they are colleagues who are just biding their time until they become "voting members" of the academy. This recognition and support is probably not needed by the majority of the independents; however, it may be crucial to future relationships with the dependents.

A Final Word

The purpose of the above discussion was not to replow the rich fields of the "who, why, how, and what" of part-time faculty; these fields have been worked rather extensively. Rather, the purpose was to help sensitize administrators to the differences between those part-time faculty members who desire full-time employment and those who are content with the status quo. To continue to treat part-time faculty members as if they are simply a part of some amorphous mass is to do a disservice to the community college and to that great and irreplaceable asset, part-time faculty. To fail to give special attention to those part-timers who want to join the teaching profession full-time is to fail the individual and the teaching profession, a failure the community college cannot afford.

References

Gappa, J. M. *Part-Time Faculty: Higher Education at a Crossroads.* ASHE-ERIC Higher Education Research Report No. 3. Washington, D.C.: The George Washington University and the Association for the Study of Higher Education, 1984.

Harris, D. A. "From the President's Perspective: Part-Time Faculty in the 1980s." In M. H. Parsons (ed.), *Using Part-Time Faculty Effectively.* New Directions for Community Colleges, no. 30. San Francisco: Jossey-Bass, 1980.

McGaughey, J. L. "Part-Time Faculty: Integrity and Integration." In D. E. Puyear and George B. Vaughan (eds.), *Maintaining Institutional Integrity.* New Directions for Community Colleges, no. 52. San Francisco: Jossey-Bass, 1985.

Parsons, M. H. (ed.). *Using Part-Time Faculty Effectively.* New Directions for Community Colleges, no. 30. San Francisco: Jossey-Bass, 1980.

George B. Vaughan is president of Piedmont Virginia Community College in Charlottesville.

Part 2. The Controversy of the Open Door

Community colleges may no longer be able to afford the idealistic vision of the open door.

The Fading Vision of the Open Door

Marc A. Nigliazzo

The most hallowed tradition of the community or junior college, the "open door," is under attack. Along with scores of other criticisms of education, a persistent questioning of the venerable open-door tradition has been evident and growing in the 1980s. And why not? Questions about the open door bring into focus two very popular concerns: standards of excellence and fiscal responsibility. As financial resources shrink, can the community college continue to justify excessive expenditure on high-risk students? As the taxpayer grows more dissatisfied with the quality of public education, can the community college continue to hope that educational exposure on a broad scale will produce enough success to justify continuation, or must it now ensure the quality of its service and the quality of its product? In preparing for the now well-known reforms of Miami–Dade, President Robert H. McCabe (Dubocq, 1981, p. 27) appropriately stated: "Society is asking for more performance and I think it has lost patience. What we have been doing simply isn't working; it has failed to meet the needs of both society and students. The public now questions the open-door concept and universities express concern over the competence of students proceeding to upper divisions. Industry is now saying, 'Give us literate people and we'll train them.'" McCabe indicates that the traditional and, admittedly, idealistic sense of mission accepted by community colleges almost from their inception has led to the present criticism and scrutiny: "We developed practices to help people gain access to higher education who might have been excluded otherwise. We tried to remove every barrier to admission so that people could come in and simply go to class. We talked about people having the right to fail, the right to choose what they want and then cut it or not. We adjusted our practices to help minority students complete the institutions. . . . The focus was on assisting students to gain certification and to achieve a sense of gratification. Often there was not equal focus on the skills or competencies required. The key became the credential rather than the achievement."

Consequently, scores of unprepared or poorly prepared students were accepted into programs that hoped to provide an avenue for success but in fact did not ensure one. When a "sense of gratification" is primary, standards of excellence will invariably suffer, and thousands of students were and continue to be graduated from community colleges each year, by certificate or diploma, without the necessary skills for competition and achievement in either the business or the academic worlds. It is thus not surprising that the public attitude has grown increasingly more negative.

The Community College Mission as Originally Defined

Of course, there was that earlier time, when a broader, more idealistic philosophy seemed not just appropriate but even necessary. When the G.I. Bill spurred the community college growth of the 1950s and the Baby Boom the growth of the 1960s, the community college was rapidly on its way to becoming all things to all people. The traditional four-year colleges, says Vaughan (1984, p. 38), "were neither physically nor philosophically prepared to deal with the sheer numbers who wanted to go to college. . . . However, the solution was at hand: The public community college was not only willing to take ill-prepared students but was also willing to spend considerable amounts of human and fiscal resources recruiting and educating them." The community college became, on the one hand, a screen for upper-level students and, on the other, an entity of its own, earnestly desiring to live up to its reputation as the most democratic of all educational institutions. Vaughan (1983, p. 7) clearly states its premise: "American democracy is founded on the belief that all people have the right and deserve the opportunity to achieve to the limits of their ability. Providing all people with open access to higher education, it is believed, will result in an educated citizenry that will work to obtain and maintain fair laws, honest government, and an economic and social system that is compatible with and supports the nation's democratic way of life."

The community college would prepare students for a four-year degree program, if that was their desire. It would respond to the needs of business and industry through occupational education. And it would produce lifelong learning opportunities for every individual. It was, as Barringer (1983, p. 56) calls it, an immensely "compassionate institution," filled with enthusiasm and promise.

A Decline in Funding and Credibility

It probably would have remained as such had college enrollments remained high and funding relatively easy to obtain, but as the American economy deteriorated in the 1970s and the Baby Boomers declined in numbers, attitudes about funding higher education began to change. Whereas the mission of the community college had once gone unchallenged, it began to be questioned. Its scope was perhaps too broad and its cost, in a time of financial constraint, hard to justify. Even community college leaders, says Vaughan (1984, p. 41), began to think it "naive . . . that colleges can be all things to all people." And he reflects upon the new pressures: "The public . . . is challenging the rationale for spending public funds on high school–level courses at postsecondary institutions. Several other factors are causing leaders to take a new look at open access, including greater demands for accountability, fewer federal dollars for the support of the social side of education, a decline in state legislators' support of community colleges . . . and a renewed emphasis on quality at all levels of education."

The ready availability of federal funding is gone. A greater burden for the support of education has been shifted to the state level and, for those colleges with local tax support, to the local level. At each source there is pressure to cut costs and to fund only what is clearly justifiable. Nelson (1980, p. 43) explains that for the community college to "maintain its claim on taxpayers' earnings, much less to increase that claim, it will no longer be sufficient to argue that an additional dollar spent on higher education will be put to good use; it will be necessary to convince the taxpayers that they will be better off if the college spends that dollar than if they do."

A tax-wary public is getting harder to convince, especially when people have come to believe that money invested in education is yielding a poor return. They are insisting that their legislators look more attentively at education, and at the community college level those legislators are finding:

- Consistent evidence of a revolving as well as an open door, with thousands of students who are admitted yearly into community colleges never completing programs of study
- Alarming expenses for remedial education, which in fact asks the taxpayer to fund for a second time the cost of a student's basic education in reading, writing, and mathematics
- An astonishing number of students who cannot complete remedial coursework but who nevertheless continue to attend "college" at the taxpayer's expense
- Curricula of diminished quality and a tendency to graduate or certify students who are still without sufficient skill to succeed in either the academic or the business worlds; four-year institutions have acknowledged this tendency by imposing junior-level entrance examinations for transfer students, thus signalling a lack of trust

- Lists of noncredit community service courses, which exhibit little resemblance to college-level content but nevertheless receive funding support.

Some, of course, have argued that there should be no alarm sounded. They have insisted that success is measured in many different ways, and that improving one's reading ability a grade level or two may be as much a success as receiving a diploma; that allowing students to "sample" higher education is an appropriate role for the community college, and that the "cooling out" syndrome is probably normal and acceptable; that the success of a community college is not measured in program completion or quality of curricula but in merely making accessible to a segment of the population the kind of instruction it wants, where and when it wants it. Vincent (1981-82, p. 13) asks, "How does one determine a price tag for this brand of success? Is one successful student worth the effort expended in attempting to help several?" And one might give an affirmative reply were the price tag lower. In spite of their idealistic tradition, community colleges must come to accept society's growing unwillingness to subsidize a fond hope for success as opposed to a greater certainty of it. Miller (1973, p. 27) captures the essence of the dilemma in stating, "Partial vocational training, partial reversal of academic deprivation, partial exposure to ideas and concepts may be as invaluable a service as turning out graduates." However, she adds, "This highly controversial question may very well be resolved not by logic, but by money."

The Tradition of the Open Door and Evidence of Its Closing

What, then, are the alternatives for community colleges as they prepare to face the criticisms brought on by financial constraints and a renewed emphasis on excellence in education? Can they maintain the open door and compete for dwindling financial resources? Can they maintain the open door and retain credibility as institutions of higher education? There is as yet no single satisfactory response. It seems that complete elimination of the open door and a return to some form of selective admissions might be in order, but perhaps that measure is unnecessarily extreme, although some modifications of the open door must certainly occur.

The open door is not easily closed for community colleges, because it has so long been a part of the community and junior college mission; it has in fact shaped that mission. "While higher education is not the only avenue through which individuals can reach their potential," explains Vaughan (1983, p. 7), "it is nevertheless a major avenue and one that is accepted by most Americans. Higher education is an especially important avenue of upward mobility for those individuals who have traditionally been denied the opportunity for higher education and thus opportunity to participate as equal partners in the American dream." And there, indeed, is the rub. Can we now completely erase that opportunity without doing irreparable damage to the community colleges and the students that they serve? Barringer (1983, p. 56) warns: "As we enter the new postindustrial age and fail to educate large numbers of people who are absolutely unprepared in the basic skills of reading, writing, and computing, our entry into that new age will leave this disenfranchised population behind. We must not create a permanent underclass of people who will not survive and will likely fall back into an abyss of despair." And he forces reflection upon the clientele of the community college:

> Our history is replete with examples of admitting people who have been discarded or ignored by other institutions. First, we took the part-time students when they were considered second-class citizens and shuffled off to an evening college so they wouldn't, allegedly, contaminate the purity of the full-time student. We took returning women when other colleges considered young people as the only authentic students, and we took the handicapped and the senior citizens before any other institution saw it as a responsibility. While attracting great numbers of students with poor academic skills, we have also attracted many who were academically talented. It is through this dynamic mix of people, a microcosm of society created by open admissions and nurtured by those of us in the system, that the community college has earned its reputation for support of our egalitarian and democratic principles in this country.

Those are strong words, which cannot be lightly dismissed by any who are a part of the community college movement in America.

But the criticisms remain, and one must agree that if the door is not to be closed, its opening must be modified. Several things are already occurring. First, to meet diminished financial support, tuition increases—in some cases substantial ones—have already become a reality. Rising tuition will undoubtedly reduce admissions, especially of the underprivileged, who are also most often the unprepared. Most of these programs have been nontraditional, high-risk occupational programs, and their elimination will further reduce the admission of high-risk students. Third, noncredit community service programs are being forced to become self-supporting through fees, which cannot help reducing interest in the programs. Fourth, efforts are under way in most states to better articulate the community college mission at the state level, in the interest of retaining if not increasing funding. However, the trade-off demanded by many state houses is most meticulous evaluation and justification of programs and documented assurance of quality. These demands, joined with the general public outcry for excellence in education, will invariably mean the elimination of weaker programs and high-risk programs and a reduction in the number of students attracted by them.

Strategies to Keep the Door Ajar

In effect, the door is already closing; admissions standards are already tightening. But how can the door be kept from slamming shut? Breneman and Nelson (1981, pp. 24-25) offer three possible strategies:

1. Return to "traditional collegiate functions—shifting focus . . . from 'community' to 'college.'" All resources would be concentrated on degree-credit programs, with each program following a very specific core curriculum. Such a course would emphasize "the more traditional values associated with higher education." The great danger is that this strategy would return community colleges to the status of junior colleges and place them even more directly in competition with senior colleges for full-time undergraduates.

2. Move more completely away from "college" to "community." This strategy would produce a "diminished role for traditional college programs and students, and an expanded role for part-time nondegree-seeking adult 'learners.'" In short, make no pretension of being a traditional college. The immediate disadvantage of this strategy is that the feelings of the times about education would almost surely work against funding.

3. Maintain the comprehensive mission, but more clearly define and articulate program priorities. However, opting for comprehensiveness is a gamble, for "colleges that lack the capacity to set limits on themselves, and to establish and defend clear priorities among activities, may see their state support diminish."

There is great uncertainty with each of these strategies. The first would eventually eliminate the uniqueness of the community college. The second would place the very concept of "college" in great jeopardy. The third has for years been the goal of most community colleges, but it seems also to have contributed to the charges now made against the cost and quality of community college education.

A Fourth Strategy: The Miami-Dade Reforms

A fourth strategy exists. It attempts to maintain comprehensiveness and a sense of the open door. However, it demands clarification of mission, program accountability, and student performance. It does not close the door, but it does in essence ask the student to justify in the foyer that he or she is worthy of admission to the parlor. This strategy is best exemplified by the "educational reform" implemented at Miami-Dade Community College. The basic concept is clarified by McCabe (Dubocq, 1981, p. 28): "There should be a controlled student flow, carefully constructed so that students proceed through the program based on their competencies and progress . . . . Students with deficiencies are required to take necessary developmental work before proceeding to programs where lack of skill could cause failure." Thus a balance of open and selective admission is achieved. All students are offered an opportunity to succeed in college, but they must prove that they merit the expenditure of the college's time and money in order to proceed through a curriculum of study. They are constantly monitored along the way, and they are offered appropriate instructional assistance, as required, but they are expected to meet the college's standards of progress within a specified period or face suspension or dismissal. McCabe explains, "There must be a point at which it is determined that the student is not going to succeed at the institution and further public investment is not justified" (p. 29).

There is little "sampling" at Miami-Dade, and the revolving door swings around less frequently. Students must perform or lose their right to open opportunity. McCabe adds: "It is absolutely essential to the continued existence of the open door that institutions establish high expectations in awarding credits, certificates, and degrees . . . . These are the currency of the institution and I am convinced that society will ultimately reject the open door if that currency is not strengthened."

In the first three years of their existence, the reforms at Miami-Dade resulted in the suspension or dismissal of over 8,000 students. Since that time, student performance has steadily improved, and dismissals continue to decline. The college has realized a savings of several million dollars because of the decline in enrollment, and it has significantly improved its credibility.

Conclusion

Besieged by the realities of declining financial support and accelerating demands for excellence in education, the open door of the community college is wavering. Success in the competition for funding demands credible, demonstrably effective programs. The community colleges can no longer say to the taxpaying public, "Trust us! We assure you that we are getting an appropriate return for your dollars." To a public clamoring for quality in education, the community colleges can no longer say, "Come to us, all of you who desire a taste of higher education. It matters not that you are ill prepared or poorly motivated." To keep the door from closing shut, community colleges must be prepared to make demands upon their students and upon themselves. They must define for themselves a mission of open access but selective progress. Through early and continuing assessment of student progress, community colleges can better determine where the expenditure of time and money is most justifiable, and they can then demonstrate that justification to the public. They need not return to the status of junior colleges; they need not yield the designation "college" and become simply community centers. They can continue to be comprehensive. Through a willingness to yield a part of that earlier idealistic vision of being all things to all people, they can keep the open door from closing. Community colleges can no longer afford that earlier vision.

References

Barringer, B. A. "Keep Open Doors Open." *Community and Junior College Journal*, 1983, *53* (4), 55-56.
Breneman, D. W., and Nelson, S. C. "The Future of Community Colleges." *Change*, 1981, *13* (5), 16-25.
Dubocq, T. "American Community Colleges in Crisis." *Change*, 1981, *13* (5), 26-31.
Miller, T. M. "The Open Door Versus the Revolving Door." *Education Digest*, 1973, *38*, 26-29.
Nelson, S. C. "Future Financing and Economic Trends." *Community and Junior College Journal*, 1980, *51* (1), 41-44.
Vaughan, G. B. "The Case for Open Access to Higher Education." *Community and Junior College Journal*, 1983, *54* (1), 7.
Vaughan, G. B. "The Community College at the Watershed: Balancing Open Access and Quality." *Change*, 1984, *16* (2), 38-44.
Vincent, W. E. "In Support of Open Admissions." *Community and Junior College Journal*, 1981-82, *52* (4), 12-13.

Marc A. Nigliazzo is vice-president and dean of instruction at Galveston College, Texas.

Traditional arguments against expensive open-admissions policies have lost their validity as the composition of the community college student body has changed radically in recent years.

Keeping the Open Door Open

William E. Demaree

"The fact is, I didn't learn much in high school." Thus begins Rondinone's (1977) article. It describes his experiences as a recent uneducated high school graduate trying for a second chance in an urban open-admissions college. Although his experiences are in most respects familiar to those of us teaching remedial courses in open-admissions colleges, Rondinone's success as a remedial student is something of an exception. Nevertheless, every developmental educator has a few similar—if less spectacular—success stories: students who arrive at a college virtually illiterate but who leave not only with new knowledge but with a love of learning as well. Rondinone and students like him vindicate, to some extent, open-admissions policies at a time when they are being assailed for their expense.

But students like Rondinone are also familiar to critics of open-admissions policies. Rondinone's description of his high school is no longer typical only of high schools in large urban areas: "The classrooms were overcrowded anyhow, and the teachers knew it. They also knew where to find me when they wanted to make weird deals: If I agreed to read a book and did an oral report, they'd pass me. So I did it and graduated with a 'general' diploma. I was a New York City public school kid" (p. 43). Critics of open-admissions policies frequently cite situations such as this and argue that colleges can no longer afford to pay for the faults of the public schools and of public school students. As college budgets shrink, students such as Rondinone, unlike "better prepared" students, may begin to disappear from our campuses.

What critics overlook is that the "second chance" students like Rondinone are no longer the primary beneficiaries of open-admissions policies. The community college student body has changed and continues to change, and the new student body invalidates the standard arguments against open-admissions policies. In fact, current trends in enrollment make open-admissions policies, as expensive as they may be, indispensable to the mission of the community college.

Arguments against open-admissions policies are familiar to us all. Some critics are simply prejudiced. Others are concerned about the fate of students who are allowed into colleges through open-admissions policies. Still others are concerned about the money, time, and personnel that open-admissions colleges devote to compensating for a problem for which public schools should have assumed responsibility.

The prejudice against open-admissions students is made painfully clear in Rondinone's essay. Rondinone, newly arrived on campus, has difficulty finding his classroom. He asks a fellow student to help him locate the building on a campus map. After pointing out that Rondinone is standing directly in front of the building he is seeking, the student asks, "Can't you read?" Another student remarks, "What do you expect from open admissions?" Rondinone reflects on the incident: "I had no idea that there were a lot of students who resented people like me, who felt that I was jeopardizing standards, destroying their institution. I had no idea. I just wanted to go to class" (p. 45). This prejudice is, unfortunately, shared by many teachers and administrators, but few critics of open admissions are motivated by a distaste for the uneducated. Some critics are more concerned about the "injustice" of allowing ill-prepared students into colleges. These critics point to the poor success rate of remedial students—students who would not be in college were it not for open-admissions policies. Every developmental educator can point with pride to a few exceptions, to students like Rondinone; having been forced to read *No Exit*, he became "obsessed with existentialism" and read Kafka, Camus, and Dostoevski on his own time (p. 46).

But Rondinone and students of his caliber *are* the exceptions. For every successful remedial student, there are a dozen who retake the same class without success two, three, or four times before finally giving up in frustration. Critics point with disdain to the rather cynical practice of taking tuition money from students who are not likely to complete the courses for which they register. Instead of benefiting from open doors, claim the critics, these students become trapped in "revolving doors"; they are the victims, not the beneficiaries, of open-door policies. And perhaps these critics have a point.

Still other critics argue that neither students nor taxpayers should pay twice for the same education. Open-admissions policies require large, expensive remedial programs; why, critics argue, should tax money and tuition be spent to teach students material they should have learned in the tenth grade or the eighth grade or, in some cases, the sixth grade? If public schools are not doing their jobs, these critics contend, we must improve the public schools.

Asking colleges to correct the problem is growing increasingly unfair, they argue, as college budgets are getting smaller and operating costs are getting larger. Open-door policies, detractors claim, are financially wasteful. And perhaps these critics also have a point.

Despite the logic of some arguments, it is important to note that community college education has changed rapidly in the last few years and that in the process many traditional arguments against open admissions have been invalidated. The most significant development is in the demographics of remedial students. Ill-prepared recent high school graduates are no longer the primary beneficiaries of open admissions.

Those of us who specialize in remedial education are well aware of this shift in the community college student body. As director of a developmental English lab, I witness the shift occurring from semester to semester. For instance, in our English Learning Center, on an average day, dozens of students with a wide range of abilities and weaknesses arrive to improve their communications skills. Some of our clients are the "typical" college students: eighteen- or nineteen-year-olds planning to transfer to another college or university in a year or two. Far too many of these students, like Rondinone, have found that their high school experiences have left them ill prepared for college work.

Sitting next to these students, however, are many who are still incorrectly referred to as nontraditional students. (Academics are notoriously slow to admit or even recognize that a new tradition has replaced an old one.) These students are familiar to any of us who teach remedial math or English or who work in tutorial centers: a twenty-nine-year-old divorced woman who needs new skills to become employable after a decade of being a housewife and mother; a thirty-year-old former drug addict who, after several years of volunteer work in drug centers, is working toward a degree in counseling; a forty-year-old mechanic, recently laid off, who is reviewing basic math and English so that he can finally get his GED; a young, well-educated Vietnamese refugee who is improving his English by taking a low-level developmental reading course; and a seventy-year-old retiree who, having been out of school for fifty years, is taking a literature course "for the fun of it."

Sound familiar? It should. Those of us who work in the English Learning Center are not the only ones facing this change in enrollment. These changes have occurred in community colleges across the nation and will continue for some time. Statistics (Association of American Colleges, 1981) are relevant here, but they come as no surprise to anyone working in our profession:

> The Carnegie Council on Policy Studies in Higher Education predicts a 23 percent decline in the traditional college-bound group of eighteen-to-twenty-four-year-olds by 1997. It maintains, however, that the impact on colleges will be partially offset by increases in participation by students twenty-five and older, by women, and by members of minority groups.

The National Center for Education Statistics forecasts that older students will account for public community college enrollment increasing from 3.9 million in 1978 to 4.2 million in 1988.

At two-year schools older students comprise 40 percent of enrollment (p. 1).

These trends have forced us to rethink and revise many of our old policies and programs, for each of these nontraditional students comes to us with a different set of problems and different goals, and none would be here if it were not for open admissions. Some, like the twenty-nine-year-old divorced mother, completed high school successfully, but because they completed their high school work some years ago, they feel that their basic skills and their "student survival skills" have grown rusty. Their performances on national college entrance tests often verify that they need remedial "refresher courses" before proceeding with college-level work.

Some, like the thirty-year-old former drug addict, saw little value in education while they were in high school; for them, as for Rondinone, high school was a wasted four years. But after years of unsatisfactory living, these students are now ready to learn.

Some, like the forty-year-old mechanic, did not complete high school at all and yet found good jobs while still quite young; but often the changing job market shatters the comfortable world that these people have known for decades. A forty-year-old uneducated unemployed mechanic often has a difficult time on the job market, for he must face younger, better-educated competitors, and unemployment is not the only potential problem. Often a promotion means that an employee must now perform new, more difficult tasks—tasks for which a poor education has left him ill equipped.

Some, like the Vietnamese refugee, are indeed well educated. In the English Learning Center, we routinely work with Vietnamese mathematicians educated in France, with Polish veterinarians, and with nurses and engineers from Latin America. These people often need from us a good ESL program or perhaps a course or two in their professional areas so that they may be licensed to work in the United States. They infrequently plan to work toward degrees.

Some, like the retiree, are developing new interests or pursuing new challenges to keep their minds active. They, too, are worried that their academic skills have grown rusty over the years, and they often complain that they are afraid of competing with younger students; they prefer remedial courses, to strengthen not only their skills but their confidence as well. Of course, their goals are simply to "take classes"; they seldom consider degrees.

These people demonstrate that we are moving toward an even more heterogeneous student body. We can no longer divide the traditional group of eighteen-to-twenty-year-olds into two groups: well prepared and ill prepared. Instead, when we now walk into classrooms, we face students of all ages. All these nontraditional students bring new types of weaknesses, new types of anxieties, and new types of strengths, and we need more, not less, funding to meet their needs.

These people also demonstrate the inadequacy of the term *junior college*. An increasing percentage of our student body no longer sees our institutions as low-rent stepping-stones to more prestigious universities; these students have different goals. For most of them, community colleges are "colleges for the community"; they are institutions that may help them move from one economic, intellectual, or social level to another. They need open-door policies because many of them would not be allowed to take classes if there were more stringent admission standards. Some of the more timorous students would even be afraid to try.

The important point is that open-door policies are no longer primarily benefiting the traditional "second chance" student. The growing numbers of nontraditional students did not necessarily graduate from their high schools ill prepared for college or for the job market. They do not come to us as personal failures or as illustrations of the failures of public schools. Their problem is not their own lack of initiative or the inadequacies of a particular institution. Their only problem is time—the time that has elapsed since they were last students.

Open-admissions policies, then are absolutely necessary to the concept of lifelong learning, a concept that more and more is determining the function and the funding of community colleges. Dropping open-admissions policies would deprive many nontraditional students of the opportunities that they currently have. Community colleges should actually be addressing the needs of these students to a greater extent by increasing the number of GED review courses, ESL courses, and re-entry programs. To hinder these students by making admission more difficult is to forsake the institution's mission and deprive it of a major source of revenue.

The programs needed to make open-admissions schools successful are costly, but their costs should be kept in perspective. The price of college programs that aid nontraditional students is small compared to that of maintaining a society laden with the uneducated, the unemployable, and the discontent. Programs that aid nontraditional students also help to alleviate costly social ills by giving people opportunities to re-enter society as workers, consumers, taxpayers, and, most important, as literate, well-educated citizens.

Critics of open admissions often overlook the intangible benefits provided to institutions. I am frequently pleased to observe the interaction between the traditional and the nontraditional students. The older students often serve as unofficial teachers, not teaching academic material but sharing the wisdom they have learned outside academe. For instance, a colleague in the history department recently told me that during a lecture on Nazi Germany a nontraditional student—an older woman who lived in Germany during the Third Reich—corrected some misinformation in the text. She then talked for an entire class period about life in Germany in the 1930s and 1940s. Her lecture, according to my colleague, was infinitely more impressive and valuable than any textbook material. What a shame, if this woman had not been allowed to enroll because of a strict admissions policy! What a shame, if her performance in a high school years ago or her performance on a college entrance test had deprived her and her fellow students of an opportunity to grow! What a shame if cost consciousness had obscured commitment to educational mission.

In short, open-admissions policies now benefit a different type of student, whose numbers are growing rapidly. These nontraditional students are not only improving the quality of their minds and their lives; they are also improving the education of our traditional students, and often they improve *us* by forcing us to test our theoretical information against their practical wisdom. Their contributions are priceless.

Rondinone shares with us his personal success as a college student, but his essay ends on a familiar, slightly sour note. He tells us that his school—City College of New York—eventually dropped its open-admissions policy: "I wonder," he says, "what will happen to those people who can learn but whose potential doesn't show in their high school average" (p. 47). I, too, wonder what will happen to these people if doors that are currently open begin to slam shut because of financial problems. I also wonder what will happen to those of us standing on the other side of those doors.

References

Association of American Colleges. *Re-entry Women: Relevant Statistics.* Washington, D.C.: Association of American Colleges, 1981.

Rondinone, P. J. "Open Admissions and the Inward 'I.'" *Change,* 1977, *9*(5), 43-47.

William E. Demaree is director of the English Learning Center at Del Mar College, Texas.

Community colleges must use increasingly limited public funds to maintain the open door, but they should also enforce rigorous academic standards.

Student Enrollment: Ways to Maintain the Commitment

Gustavo A. Mellander

In troubled economic times, the clearest way to maintain a commitment to students is to do what many believe is counter to community college mores. That is, quite simply, to raise academic standards, to demand more of students and colleagues on campus, and to remain open to the particular needs of all constituencies.

If we really want to help students, if that is our major commitment, the way to help them is to raise academic standards. This does not mean that we close the open door; open admissions should continue to exist. What cannot exist is guaranteed graduation. We should not allow students to graduate until we have assured ourselves that students have learned what we say we have taught them.

The community college differs from the traditional liberal arts college in its relationship to the community and in its emphasis on career or continuing education; but at the heart of the community college should be a solid general and basic education for all students, no matter what their final plans. The college should be staffed with men and women dedicated to their students and to the creation and maintenance of the highest possible academic standards. Academic rigor and community service through career education are not mutually exclusive.

If we in the community colleges wish to regain or retain public trust, we must give evidence that we are working to earn that trust. We dare not permit students to coast along without written assignments, living in a world of computerized, short-answer examinations. We dare not foster grade inflation or a "when I feel like it" attendance pattern. We dare not request public funds for community colleges that do not function for the community, for its welfare and development. Especially when funds are limited, we must prove that we are doing our jobs well. We best help students by establishing rigorous standards and then helping students to achieve them. We do not help them one iota by granting them a tinsel diploma they have not earned. In fact, we cripple them and defraud the taxpayer.

True, it may well come to pass that when standards are raised, there will be a drop in enrollment. That is what happened at Passaic County College when we instituted higher academic standards in 1976. Our enrollment dropped by nearly 20 percent in one year. However, within two years, our enrollment not only recovered but surpassed our previous record, and it has increased every year since then. In summary, once it is clear to all that a community college does indeed have high academic standards, students come, study, have a different attitude toward education, and perform better. Further, employers look favorably upon the college and employ more of its graduates. At the same time, four-year colleges are eager to accept transferring students. Even local politicians jump on the bandwagon.

Perhaps a bit of history of how one institution addressed the issue will help. One of the nineteen New Jersey community colleges, Passaic County College, was chartered in 1968. At that time, it was projected that enrollment would zoom to 10,000 students within five years. The college was housed during those early days in a very old and dilapidated surplus telephone company building. From the very beginning, the college had academic problems. The college's reputation suffered, and enrollment suffered as well. In the spring of 1975, seven years after its founding, the college had fewer than 900 students.

The Scene in 1975

In 1975, Passaic County College provided a classic textbook example of how a college can go wrong—how it can go wrong academically, and how it will pay for it both politically and financially.

1. By 1975, the college had adopted virtually every innovative idea that was in vogue at that time—for instance, in the area of grades. It was considered unfair, unkind, and discriminatory for students to receive "punitive" grades. Therefore, the grades of D and F had been abolished. They could not be earned, could not appear on a transcript. They simply did not exist. Needless to say, nobody was ever placed on academic probation, and nobody was ever suspended for academic reasons. Such "medieval trappings" simply did not exist, for they were considered primitive and punitive.

2. It was also decided by all parties that there should not be any essay examinations—none at all, not even in the liberal arts. All examinations, quizzes, midterms, and finals had to be either multiple-choice or true-and-false questions.

3. The open door was as wide as a barn door. Students could enroll in any and every program on a first-come, first-served basis. Hundreds of students, who did not have the rudimentary education necessary to succeed in highly technical programs, were nevertheless admitted into those programs. Clearly, disaster loomed—and it struck. Only 36 percent of the college's nursing graduates passed the state boards. That is a polite way of stating that some 64 percent did not pass; 64 percent of the students had invested two or three years of their lives at the institution, had been duly certified by the college, and were unable to pass the state boards four weeks after they graduated!

4. Even the proposed new buildings came under the "innovation" wing of "academic architecture." The proposed buildings were to be a series of miniclassrooms, none to accommodate more than twenty students. Many were to be even smaller. The state refused to accept the idea and refused to fund the buildings four different times.

5. Regional accreditation still had not been achieved after seven years. In fact, the Middle States accrediting agency questioned whether or not it should revoke the institution's candidacy status. A ranking official of the New Jersey Department of Higher Education called the college "an academic disgrace." Several state evaluation visits were conducted, and they hinted that the college should close down.

6. The local press caught a whiff of the institution's drift and wrote a series of exposés. The general public became extremely hostile. The college became a political football. It became a place for politicians to visit and hold press conferences focusing on the college's many academic shortcomings. Political careers were launched, and from that flowed a drastic reduction in the college's capital and operating budgets.

What to do?

The College's Board of Trustees decided to select a new president. I arrived in April of 1975. Within a few months, it seemed to me that the most efficient course of action was to close the college, dismiss everybody (including me), let the dust settle for a year or two, and then reopen. I presented that proposal to the chancellor of higher education, the college board, and the county government officials. It was reviewed and seriously considered but ultimately rejected on the grounds that the college was so widely disrespected that, were it to close, it would never open again. The task then became to rebuild from within. Shortly thereafter, a series of meetings was held with faculty, students, administrators, and the general community. Out of these came many recommendations and many suggested reforms, and 95 percent of the reforms ultimately implemented came directly from those groups.

It was decided that although a community college has many obligations, many missions, and many diverse constituencies, it was first and foremost an academic institution. That was to be the vibration to which we would respond. That would be our measuring stick. Everything else would be secondary, everything else would be responded to at a lower level.

Traditional grading was established: A through F. At the same time, we discouraged pass/fail grading, for we wanted to encourage and distinguish between excellence and adequacy. We also asked every teacher to become an English teacher. Every teacher, regardless of his or her discipline, was asked to help our students become more proficient in using the written and spoken word. Every teacher was encouraged and asked to employ essay examinations. True-and-false and multiple-choice exams were discouraged. We expected all teachers to demand the very best of their students—and of themselves.

To help our students gain needed skills, we established a writing-across-the-curriculum program. Its goal was to incorporate a writing component in every single course and, when possible, to coordinate shared assignments between various disciplines. Students majoring in business administration, for example, would find their English teachers selecting theme assignments relating to their chosen careers. Cooperation and coordination among the teachers was essential, and it would come to pass only if fully and properly supported by the administration.

We also established a traditional probation and suspension system. A year later, and therefore after students had been given fair warning and an opportunity to adjust to the new reality, we implemented them. A third of the student body was either suspended or placed on probation, including half the college basketball team. We were not at all pleased with the high number of suspensions and decided not to publicize our actions. When one of the basketball players complained to the press, however, the college was in for a pleasant surprise: Newspapers covering the story wrote favorable articles about our attempts to maintain academic standards—even for athletes. We went from disdain and criticism to praise and encouragement in a single year; people became aware that our open-admissions policy does not imply lack of standards and that we are not willing to waste the taxpayers' money.

What else did we do? First, we insisted that all faculty members advise students, work during registration, and adhere to their scheduled office hours. We also closed the "academic cafeteria." Full-time students could no longer select either majors or courses in a willy-nilly fashion. There is now a coherent core of information that all students must master before graduating. A free-flowing, unstructured system of selecting courses does not help the vast majority of community college students. They need more professional direction, and it is our duty to provide it.

Second, we examined every course in the catalogue to assure ourselves of its academic vigor. Many were upgraded. New syllabi followed, along with departmental responsibilities to monitor the upgrading process. Further, a mechanism was established to evaluate each academic program every three years. In the 1960s we drifted away from the rigor inherent in and necessary to a college education. We tended not to ask enough of our students. There is a discipline to learning; the so-called old-fashioned requirements of punctuality, attendance, homework, and concentrated time on tasks are absolutely essential.

Third, we established an assessment process for every incoming student, to determine how he or she could best be served. As is true of most community college students, many were lacking the basic skills to successfully address college-level courses. To help them, we established a learning center. It is a demanding program. Students must attend five days a week, from 9:00 P.M. to 4:00 P.M., and homework is an integral daily component of the program. Attendance is monitored—three unexcused absences make the student subject to suspension. Tardiness is not tolerated, either. In effect, we mirror the expectations of the professional world, and thus we genuinely "open the door." Now, depending on their needs, students are placed in mathematics, reading, writing, and speech laboratories. A vast majority need the entire array. Since its inception, the program has had some magnificent successes, and some very disappointing failures as well. Some students raised their reading/writing/mathematics competencies two full years after a semester of concentrated study. Many have gone on to graduate from college. The program is very time-consuming and expensive, but the alternative is far more dismal.

Fourth, Passaic now collects, prints, and publishes all grades. The listed number of A's, B's, C's, D's, and F's each faculty member awards forms a very revealing document, particularly useful when published and widely distributed. Considerable peer pressure tends to concentrate on those teachers who seem to congregate at either extreme: those who consistently give only A's or those who give only F's. It is a most effective way of addressing grade inflation, as well as reality.

A fifth reform was the establishment of a student academic achievement committee. We were careful to call it *student academic achievement* because our main goal was not retention; our main goal was to help students discover their academic potential and develop plans to achieve it. Some have been counseled to transfer to other institutions; others have been counseled to remain at Passaic, in their majors or in new majors, or to spend more time acquiring the basics they lack. It is important not to worry about retention per se; colleges must help students to do what is best for them. This is a true opening of the door.

Finally, we instituted a comprehensive tutoring program for which the college picks up the entire cost. We also established a mandatory essay examination that all students must pass before they graduate. It is offered four times a year and may be taken by freshmen, although students normally are not encouraged to take it until they have completed two semesters of freshman English. Students write an essay on a given topic, such as "Who is your favorite historical figure, and why?" The examination lasts two hours. If students fail, the college helps by assigning a tutor to help them overcome their weaknesses. Intense assessment and tutoring follow to help students—all without any charge to them. It is an expensive and time-consuming program, but it focuses everybody's—faculty, students, and administrators—attention on the acquisition of college-level competency.

Two final thoughts: First, colleges—like other businesses or institutions—must keep close to the consumers. We must constantly search for what students really want and need. Clearly, it does not mean turning colleges into non-academic institutions. Students want to succeed, and they know or can be taught that knowledge, difficult as it may be to acquire, affords them their best opportunity to achieve their ambitions. One way to be more receptive to student needs is to offer classes at times most convenient to them. Passaic instituted a weekend college, whereby students could pursue full majors by attending classes on Friday evening and on Saturday and Sunday afternoon. It took extraordinary coordination and financial commitment during the first two or three years, for classes were small at the beginning. What I found most satisfying was not only that 900 students (most of them new to the college) enrolled but also that 82 percent of them told us that, given their other obligations, they could not have pursued college education except during those weekend times. Now, that is opening the door and serving the community!

Second, faculty must be given full support; their academic decisions have to be respected and not overturned. The previous administration, if a large number of students dropped out of classes, berated faculty members with such questions as "What's wrong? Aren't you a *good* teacher?" We reversed that. We assured teachers that we expected them to maintain academic standards, period, and that they would be supported by the administration fully and completely. An incident during our early years illustrates the point. A teacher approached the academic dean and stated that she had caught a student cheating on an examination. She wondered if she could discipline him and whether the administration would object. The dean assured her—as diplomatically as his blood pressure allowed him to—that he would support her decision. She then gave the student an F for that test. Later, the student went to see the dean to complain. After listening to the student, the dean said that he did indeed believe the teacher was wrong. Instead of failing the examination, the student should have received an F for the entire course, and he, the dean, was going to award him that grade. After gathering his composure and failing to change the dean's mind, the student asked if there was anyone else he could appeal to. The dean said he could appeal to the president, but that he was sure the president would go one step further and suspend the student from the college. The student never sought out the president. More important, the word spread throughout the college. The faculty felt much more secure—as indeed they should—in their ability to make academic judgments.

Neither Playgrounds Nor Prisons

The institution of realistic academic reforms gave the faculty the necessary authority to evaluate students' work and achievements. It also gave students themselves a far greater challenge than many had faced before, a conscious opportunity to develop habits that lead to success. Colleges should not be prisons, but neither should they be playgrounds. Hard work, self-discipline, and dedication should be hallmarks of all colleges. Education is a serious and costly business. Once we make promises to students, we should be prepared to keep them, however great the cost.

Our decisions at Passaic were necessary, although hardly easy to make. We risked serious financial constraints, public animosity, and widespread distortion of our purpose and goals. All of those decisions, however, were preferable to maintaining an educational charade. To our delight, we found that enrollments increased, faculty supported the decisions, and the public offered widespread support. Even our students indicated their pleasure in attending a community college that was dubbed a non-nonsense institution. We were on our way to establishing an academically sound institution.

Overcoming the Stigmas

Although I am loath to generalize, I am convinced that community college education, if it is to retain public confidence and maintain its commitment to students, must undertake a return to rigorous humanistic education for all students, whether they are traditional or nontraditional. There are too many canards that community colleges are "dumping grounds" for incompetent students. If we are to overcome the stigma of inferiority, we should ensure that students in community colleges are encouraged to achieve their best, to develop a sense of pride and accomplishment. They should see themselves as part of a growing community of educated professionals who can bring to their work full and rich educational backgrounds. A firm stress on academic standards, on the ethic of success, will go a long way toward restoring what we have lost. Community colleges should educate the whole person, not simply train or make up for secondary school deficiencies. Let us remember that whether a two-year college calls itself a community college, a county college, or a county community college, one word remains constant: *college*. A college is a place to educate and elevate the mind and spirit, and people are willing to pay for that.

Gustavo A. Mellander, former president of Passaic Community College, is chancellor of West Valley-Mission Community College District in California.

Part 3. Retrenchment and Quality

The commitment to quality education in the midst of declining enrollments and budgets requires community colleges to consider more than student credit hours and costs per student when cutting back programs.

Maintaining Commitment to Quality Education

John M. McGuire
Eldon Miller

Committed to providing accessible, comprehensive programs of merit, community colleges experienced remarkable growth during the past two decades. Now, a declining traditional college-age population, greater competition from four-year colleges and universities for the traditional and even the nontraditional student, and diminishing budgets are challenging community colleges to reaffirm their commitment to quality education. While enrollments have leveled off or declined, operating costs have increased. Public colleges must convince legislatures to sustain budgets at existing levels or increase them to ensure excellence. Their funding emphasis has shifted from quantity to quality, from touting new programs and increased student credit hours to protecting and enhancing institutional quality. In the meantime, government leaders are insisting on "accountability," declaring that additional funds will not automatically be forthcoming. Rather, the colleges must put their houses in order by eliminating nonessential and redundant programs while improving the quality of what remains. In meeting these challenges, community colleges will be securing their mission and identity within the American higher education system and within their local communities.

Quality

With open-door accessibility as a central part of their mission, community colleges from their beginnings have been confronted with the challenge of quality, sometimes referred to as a problem of "image." They have discerned that much of the difficulty with quality rests with its definition. Palmer (1983-84), reviewing the literature on quality, identified five indicators of quality at the community college: institutional resources, instructional and administrative organization and processes, student outcomes, values added to students, and curricular structure and emphasis. Institutional resources, organizational structure, and curriculum are traditional measures, often used by regional accrediting agencies, of quality in colleges and universities.

The emphasis on student outcomes and value added is the newest measurement of quality and is in part a response to the call for "accountability." It remains controversial. For example, Enarson (1983) minced few words in characterizing this input-output approach as "nonsense . . . bush-league economics . . . [and] zeal for quantification carried to its inherent and logical absurdity." He suggests instead that the qualities that define us at our best and worst cannot be measured, referring to "love, compassion, patriotism, simple endurance in the face of adversity" (p. 8). Perhaps the effort to measure quality is similar to the dilemma of Justice Potter Stewart when he was called upon to define pornography. He concluded that he could not intelligibly define it, but he knew it when he saw it.

Nevertheless, the concerns of many governors and state legislatures for quality and accountability are being translated into mandated competency testing for entry into college programs, for transfer from lower-level to upper-level status in college, for entrance into a profession, and for continued certification within a profession. With all this competency testing will come the obvious temptation to measure institutions from the relative performance of their students on the standardized tests. We may emerge from the effort to define quality only to discover that the tests have already defined it for us.

The Focus on Curriculum

Whatever the outcome of these competency-testing initiatives, for many community colleges the advent of reduced funding in the 1980s has served to focus the issue of quality on their comprehensive curricula. For the past three decades, community college management has centered on expansion. Richardson and Martens (1981) warn that this cannot continue; community colleges simply cannot do everything. Many community colleges have already been forced to choose a particular curricular emphasis (Cross, 1982). Cohen and Brawer (1982a) noted that, in general, community colleges in the 1970s shifted their curricular emphasis from a predominantly college-transfer, liberal arts function to a greater concentration on career, developmental, and continuing education programs.

Such shifts in student demands and in curricular emphasis did not always constitute a mortal threat to other programs in the college. During the earlier periods of growth, these changes could be accommodated simply by adjusting the slices of the larger economic pie among the various departments. While the departments with declining enrollments might not see their budgets grow, at least their budgets were not slashed or eliminated. In the 1980s, faced with constant or declining budgets, administrators are confronted with the dilemma that growth in any one area may be accomplished only through a reduction or elimination of some other department in the college. However, if community colleges allow their collegiate function, with its liberal and performing arts, to become a casualty of tight budgets and enrollment trends, then their very mission and identity will have been altered. Comprehensive community colleges may find themselves in the process of becoming community services agencies or technical institutes.

That, indeed, has been suggested as the path to survival for community colleges. Morgan (1981) maintains that community colleges simply cannot compete successfully with four-year colleges and universities in a tight market for traditional students. He suggests that those community colleges emphasizing college-transfer programs will suffer the most during a period of general population decline and that the community colleges suffering the least will be those emphasizing vocational, nonacademic, and community services programs.

The increased competition for students and the fiscal restraints of the 1980s have confronted community colleges with fundamental questions concerning their mission and their curricula. Cohen and Brawer (1982b) note with concern that a number of community colleges have already abandoned the collegiate function altogether, while others have been restricted by governing boards or state legislatures to offering little beyond career programs. It would indeed be ironic if, in an effort to enhance quality by eliminating low-enrollment (or ''weak'') programs, community colleges ceased to provide a curriculum focused on higher learning.

Some Quality Considerations

Maintaining the breadth and quality of an institution's curriculum, when confronted with shifts in enrollment and declining budgets, requires balance and judgment. Some activities will have to be curtailed. As community colleges evaluate their programs in relationship to mission, budgets, student credit hours generated, and costs per student, they might also include consideration of the following:

Mission. Before cutting any program in the face of declining enrollments and budgets, a community college must reassess its particular mission as a comprehensive community college, and then evaluate the threatened program in the light of that program's relationship to the centrality of the college's mission. During a period of tight budgets, the temptation is of course to cut weak (that usually means low-enrollment) programs so that higher-demand (that is, strong) programs may grow. For community colleges, priding themselves on their flexibility and their responsiveness to market forces in higher education, this is a strong temptation. It is a survival tactic, "feed the strong and starve the weak," commonly associated with the economics of the marketplace. However, a simple acceptance of market trends is not sufficient. A college's curriculum is the public statement of its values, its priorities, and even its identity as an institution.

A college should not eliminate a program simply because it is supposedly weak. A college may need to eliminate a program that is no longer needed by the community or one that is not central to the college's mission, but if a so-called weak program is deemed to be needed by the community or to be central to the college's mission, the response of the college should be to support the program, revitalize it, and improve its quality. Quality improvements, which may include more imaginative design, teaching, and marketing of the program, can result in increased enrollment, particularly if the need for the program has been correctly identified.

The Collegiate Function with Business and Industry. Higher learning, or the collegiate function, need not be limited to the transfer program. Communication and problem-solving skills, critical thinking and reflection, and human sensitivity and understanding are qualities in high demand by employers everywhere. All career programs should include a substantial component of such higher learning in their curricula. Cohen and Brawer (1982b) outline a service industry and small-business entry-level program centered around such skills.

At Parkersburg Community College our program advisory boards and our planning forums, composed of business and civic leaders, have repeatedly emphasized the need for improved communication, problem solving, and learning skills. Representatives of industry have placed reduced emphasis on the need for specific technical skills, particularly in light of the rather rapid pace of change in many of these areas. As a result, the college has revised a number of its engineering technology programs to include more scientific theory, mathematics, and communications courses.

The strong links that community colleges have established with business and industry can also provide an avenue for marketing their more collegiate courses. Many industries today are willing to support, often with tuition reimbursements, all educational pursuits of their employees, whether directly job-related or not. With the nearly continuous upgrading and retraining associated with employment today, such efforts by employers support the concept of continuous or lifelong learning and can result in more productive and adaptive workers. Also, special history or economics or other liberal arts courses may be geared to a particular industry and offered to the firms in that industry, perhaps to be taught at the plant site. For example, Parkersburg Community College has developed a plastics-oriented organic chemistry course (with our basic chemistry course as a prerequisite) for the nontechnical employees of the area's plastics industries, enabling a better understanding of the companies' processes and products.

Image and Reputation. The contribution of each program to the image and reputation of the college should be assessed. Community colleges, with a high proportion of commuting and part-time students, are constantly challenged to create among their students a sense of the college community and an identification with the college. The liberal and performing arts program can contribute to the creation of a college-life environment within the college. For example, at Parkersburg Community College the state championships and national achievements of its forensic teams, the performances and tours of its chorale, the exhibition on campus of the works of its photography and three-dimensional art programs, and its annual lecture and performing arts series all contribute significantly to the college's image with students and the community. Furthermore, the college's foundation contributes each year to the purchase of works of student art to become part of the college's permanent collection.

Prospective majors in all areas, whether in computer science or engineering, are informed that their extracurricular interests need not be abandoned should they choose to attend Parkersburg Community College. The humanities division regularly reviews the extracurricular activities listed on all scholarship applications and then contacts each prospective student directly concerning the opportunities for continuing such activities while at Parkersburg Community College. Although these arts programs are not large-enrollment programs by any means, they make a significant contribution to the recruiting of students in all programs at the college. When combined with the college's accessibility and low cost, these programs can enable a community college to compete successfully with four-year colleges and universities for the traditional student.

Need. The need for the program in the community and the availability of similar programs are important considerations. For example, in communities in which the community college is the sole institution of higher learning, the citizens are likely to expect the college to exercise a prominent role in cultural activities and performing arts. Should this not be expected, the college may be compelled to exercise leadership in informing citizens of the importance of such programs and of the means by which the community can assist the college in providing these activities. Such programs can be designated strong components of the college's community service function as well as central parts of its curriculum. In contrast, community colleges in large urban areas with accessible four-year colleges and universities may need to identify a more specialized or more narrowly focused role in this area. In either case, cooperative arrangements with community theater groups, museums, art centers, and choral societies can provide a rich source of students, as well as an opportunity to share faculty, facilities, and programs. Also, corporations and businesses are often willing to contribute to a college's public lecture and performing arts programs.

Long-Range Considerations. Community colleges should acknowledge the goal of maintaining academic quality over time. Colleges need to respond to shifts in demand, and community colleges have established themselves as masters of the art, but such market responsiveness carries with it the risk of the college's being whipped about by the winds of fashion and fad. In addition to monitoring the market, a community college needs to determine which courses or programs are essential to the integrity, continuity, and stability of its curriculum and endeavor to protect them. It should also assess the relative ease of restoring a program, should it be eliminated. A study of small, four-year liberal arts colleges (Lawrence, 1984) found that the more resilient colleges maintained a strong and clear sense of identity, made major decisions on the basis of that identity, and were more likely to make marginal rather than major changes in programs.

Paring Back. Across-the-board cuts—using pruning shears, rather than wielding the ax—may be the best way to preserve the quality and breadth of the curriculum while weathering the current budget crisis. Program elimination at best is a tricky and unpopular endeavor. No matter how fair, it will be seen as arbitrary and unjust by many. Faculty in the liberal arts, as Enarson (1983) observes, have little confidence in quantification, particularly the kind that commonly accompanies program reviews. Because program elimination is damaging to institutional morale, Bowen (1983) concludes that across-the-board cuts not only are colleges' typical response to financial retrenchment but also are the appropriate way for colleges to respond. Such acts are more likely to be perceived as fair and respectful of the sense of trust and tradition within the academic community.

Cutbacks, rather than elimination, can take many forms. For example, at Parkersburg Community College we have been able in part to maintain the quality and breadth of our music and art curricula by sharing the instructional assignments of one of our art instructors and one of our music instructors with nearby four-year colleges. As a result, the college can continue to provide courses in specialized areas of these disciplines taught by a full-time professional instructor, but at a substantially reduced cost. The benefits, of course, are the same for each of the four-year colleges that have contracted for a portion of the instructor's time.

Academic Standards. The maintenance of high academic standards is often unrelated to budgets or funding variations. Requiring a strong general education core (not awarding degree credit for precollege courses) and enforcing reasonable standards of academic progress are components of a respectable curriculum that are not directly related to funding. Certainly, no community college should lower academic standards in an effort to attract or retain students; such a response would prove self-defeating and particularly untimely in light of recent national and regional reports calling for increased rigor and coherence in curricula and in degree standards. Rather, strong developmental programs will both provide the necessary skills for underprepared students and reduce the rate of attrition without lowering academic standards or limiting access. Although credit is often awarded in precollege courses for purposes of accounting and funding, these credits should not apply toward an associate degree.

Community colleges commonly have developmental courses in mathematics, English composition, and reading. As community colleges address quality improvements in career-technical programs, they might consider reclassifying some entry-level technical skill courses as precollege/developmental courses. In many cases these courses duplicate those taught at secondary career centers. Community colleges can replace these entry-level technical courses with additional higher-level skill courses, thereby raising the quality and skills within the career-technical program. At the same time, access to associate degrees for the underprepared student can be established by way of developmental programs in math, English, and reading that include a parallel series of entry-level technical courses. To the extent that community colleges can increase the skill levels of their career programs while at the same time eliminating costly duplication, they will provide a strong response to the call for accountability. This in turn should enhance requests for increased funding for other cost-related improvements across the curriculum.

Summary. The commitment to quality education in the midst of declining enrollments and budgets demands that community colleges consider more than student credit hours generated and costs per student when cutting back programs or courses. No responsible community college should maintain a cavalier disregard for enrollments and market trends, but the commitment to a quality curriculum necessitates the consideration of other factors as well. When cuts have to be made, a college must evaluate programs on the basis of the college's mission; the needs of the community; the relationship of the program to the college's overall image and reputation; the college's long-term and short-term needs; the role of the collegiate function; and the benefits of simply cutting back, whenever possible, rather than eliminating. The protection of essential programs can entail sharing faculty with other institutions, developing cooperative arrangements with community agencies and cultural groups, and eliciting support from civic and business leaders. With these efforts and considerations, community colleges can emerge from the current crisis with their identity, integrity, and quality intact.

References

Bowen, H. R. "The Art of Retrenchment." *Academe*, 1983, *69* (1), 21-24.
Cohen, A. M., and Brawer, F. B. *The American Community College.* San Francisco: Jossey-Bass, 1982a.
Cohen, A. M., and Brawer, F. B. "The Community College as College: Should the Liberal Arts Survive in Community Colleges?" *Change*, 1982b, *14* (2), 39-42.

Cross, K. P. "Teaching in Community Colleges." In *Promoting Great Teaching: A Staff Development Imperative. Institute on Staff Development. May 25-28, 1982. Proceedings.* Austin, Tex.: University of Texas, Program in Community College Education, 1982. (ED 221 250)

Enarson, H. L. "Quality—Indefinable but Not Unattainable." *Educational Record*, 1983, *64* (1), 7-9.

Lawrence, B. "Beyond the Bottom Line: Good Managers Look to Results." *Community and Junior College Journal*, 1984, *54* (5), 21-23.

Morgan, D. A. "Maintaining Quality in Troubled Times: The Community College Perspective." Paper presented at Pacific Rim Association for Higher Education annual conference, Seattle, October 13-14, 1981. (ED 214 483)

Palmer, J. C. "How Is Quality Measured at the Community College?" *Community College Review*, 1983-84, *11* (3), 52-62.

Richardson, R. C., Jr., and Martens, K. J. "Planning for Quality Instruction in the '80s." *Community College Frontiers*, 1981, *9* (3), 51-54.

John M. McGuire is dean of instruction at Aurora Community College, Denver, Colorado.

Eldon Miller is president of Parkersburg Community College, West Virginia.

As financial woes for colleges mount, there is a clear and persuasive argument for selective program elimination to counter economic definciencies.

Weak Programs: The Place to Cut

Ronald J. Temple

The need for community colleges to exercise prudent judgment in academic programming has never been greater. The 1980s have been a sobering experience for higher education. Tuition costs have risen, inflation has played havoc with the academic budget, and the availability of financial aid to students has declined. Unless creative, careful, and sometimes drastic action is taken, the critically important flexibility that higher education requires in order to be responsive to changing needs will be lost.

Institutions have responded differently to the problems of rising costs and enrollment declines. Some, indeed many, institutions have prostituted themselves, to such a point that the drive for students has clouded their academic mission. For example, in an attempt to attract students, many community colleges have violated the curricular intergrity of their institutions. "Smorgasbord" curricular designs have provided such a multitude of options that they have smothered the precision necessary for quality education. While flexibility in a curriculum is desirable, courses must be constructed in such a way as to meet certain academic goals and expectations. Such ends have been lost in the smorgasbord programs. More important, "graduates" of such programs have met frustration in attempting to match their credentials with the expectations of employers.

Other institutions have responded to financial and enrollment difficulties by virtually eliminating or substantially reducing academic access requirements for potential students and by correspondingly increasing frustration for faculty

B. W. Dziech (Ed.), *Controversies and Decisions in Hard Economic Times.* New Directions for Community Colleges, no. 53. San Francisco: Jossey-Bass, March 1986.

who have not known how to respond to nontraditional students. The overwhelming majority of institutions that have embarked on this course have been baccalaureate colleges exploring every alternative in order to survive. Unfortunately, they have not learned the lesson of the two-year college, which has clearly set the example for curriculum design for underprepared students. These misguided institutions have conflicting values (elitism versus survival), while most quality two-year colleges learned early that special preparation was required for instructing the underprepared student.

A carefully constructed curriculum that prepares students to meet expectations at the college level requires considerable expertise on the part of the faculty and administrators who direct such programs. Success does not come overnight, and—most important—it does not come without considerable expense. But the lesson of the community college is clear. There are experts in the field of developmental education, and if resources are available, and the correct and proper principles are designed into the curriculum, underprepared students can meet high expectations.

Nevertheless, institutions that opened their doors solely because of financial exigencies, and did not understand the extensive effort required to meet the needs of underprepared students, find themselves in a dilemma. In some cases the nature of the institution has changed uncontrollably; in others, students have met with such frustration that the open door has become essentially a revolving door. What, then, does higher education do when faced with the need to provide quality education to a more heterogeneous student body in an era of economic uncertainty?

The academy must consider a variety of modalities in response to declining resources and increasing expense. Clearly, frivolous courses have no substantial place in an academic curriculum. The issue is whether or not colleges can afford to keep courses and programs that do not carry their weight in an economic as well as an academic sense.

The Across-the-Board Strategy

In the 1980s, many institutions have taken the easy way out in response to declining budgets. The internal process of budgetary decisions has resulted in an increasingly politicized faculty and staff. Presidents and deans have been ostracized and scorned for making "hard decisions." Votes of "no confidence" by faculty and staff and petitions to boards of directors challenging the decisions of administrators have become commonplace. While faculties have actively sought to participate in the governing process, they have resisted and refused the responsibility of making difficult decisions. They have been willing to assess theoretically the long-term needs of their institutions but unwilling to put theory into practice and admit the need for painful choices.

To avoid conflict, many administrators, ultimately responsible for responding to the budget crisis, began to take the easy route, and thus began across-the-board budget cuts. Nothing could have been more harmful to the long-range future of higher education than the attempt to put everyone in the same boat.

In fact, it was the reverse strategy that was needed. The times required not across-the-board budget reductions but a selective process of program elimination. While the across-the-board approach to budget reductions eliminates certain short-range pressures, it also creates major long-range crises. For example, a 5 percent across-the-board reduction gives the impression that it is fair and equitable. In truth, it may be neither. Some potentially outstanding programs may already be grossly underfunded and therefore initially unequal to their other partners. To cut programs that are already underfunded may cause irreparable harm to the quality of programs in the future. In every kind of institution, some programs are, for various reasons, financially better off than others. Thus, it is unwise to assume that all programs are equal in the quality of their financial support and can therefore assume equal budget reduction without some suffering considerable harm.

Again, some programs may be better funded than they ought to be. The across-the-board approach to budget reduction does not result in the type of introspection that responsible budget reduction should encourage. If programs already have surplus income, they are not forced to make the same qualitative judgments required of other programs. If they are fat cats, they simply become less fat, not necessarily better.

The across-the-board approach to budget reduction has an even more devastating impact on academic programming. Such an approach basically disregards the issues of quality and importance of the program. If we truly believe that quality is a constant and a given, and that everything else is important but subordinate, then across-the-board reductions mean what they say. They must be accomplished without regard to quality, because the concept allegedly demands equity of treatment, although—as shown above—such treatment is seldom if ever equitable.

Even though assessment of quality can be very difficult, it must be done. The major flaw of the across-the-board approach to budget reduction is that it cannot make qualitative distinctions. The model, by its very nature, rejects such distinctions, and the harm of this approach to academic programming is serious and lasting. Under this approach, quality programs may very well become weak programs. Shrinking resources will force them to take shortcuts, to be less adventurous, and to pursue strategies of survival rather than excellence. Across-the-board reductions often force quality programs to become mediocre programs, but weak programs are already weak and are therefore less altered by budget limitations. Weak programs are already accustomed to lower expectations, and the overall condition of such programs does not change when reductions occur. Thus, weak programs pull quality programs toward their level. Obviously, then, there is a clear and persuasive argument for selective program eliminations, rather than for across-the-board reductions.

Selective Program Elimination

The advantages of selective program elimination in the time of budgetary constraints are many. If such an approach is taken, it is possible not only to maintain quality programs but, under proper conditions, also to improve and strengthen them. Probably the most significant advantage of selective program elimination is that, if it is done correctly, it requires an institution to raise critical questions relating to values and mission, while across-the-board reductions reduce the pressure for such discussions to occur. The focus on mission and values can bring rationality to the decision-making process.

For instance, a community college that values the open-admissions principle will probably place more priority on developmental curriculum than would a highly selective baccalaureate institution. While both institutions might have developmental needs, the mission and values that the community college holds dear would support the maintenance of a well-structured but expensive developmental program, and the college would thus be compelled to sacrifice other program offerings deemed to be less essential to its mission.

The inherent requirement for maintaining commitment and excellence in academic matters is frequent introspection. Too often, such activity occurs only in times of crisis. At least if the strategy of program elimination is adopted in a crisis, an institution can use that opportunity to rededicate and recommit itself to its primary mission. Such an approach certainly reduces the likelihood of providing only a smorgasbord curriculum and of neglecting the basic values of the institution.

In addition to the issues of mission and values, the specific criteria used to finalize a judgment about academic programs become increasingly important. Certain conditions should prevail in making decisions about program elimination. Although it may appear to be harsh and heartless to the faculty, the prevailing criterion must be based on what is most advantageous for the student. The issue of faculty and staff careers is legitimate, but in an academic environment these considerations must be secondary to quality instruction for students. While there may be several options available to assist faculty and staff who might be affected by program elimination, the primary commitment must be to students, for whom the institution exists in the first place.

The issue of equal educational opportunity, too, is better addressed by program elimination than by the across-the-board approach to budget reduction. Many of the newest and most underfunded programs are designed for nontraditional students and are most likely to suffer under across-the-board reductions. While access to education may be provided in different ways by our institutions, they must all maintain a commitment to the principle of access. Creating artificially high admissions standards, as many states are now in the process of doing, serves only to cause unfair competition when increased admissions standards are juxtaposed with the principle of equal educational opportunity. Admissions standards do not ensure quality; exit standards speak to quality. Program elimination, rather than across-the-board reduction, better equips institutions to provide equal educational opportunity for students. The commitment to equal access must not be allowed to become a casualty of budget reduction.

Another criterion to be considered in determining which programs should stay and which should be eliminated is quality. Criteria must be established to judge the quality of academic programs. It is unlikely that a program would ever judge itself poor in quality if it knew that such a judgment might ultimately result in its elimination. Since it is unreasonable to assume that a program would recommend self-elimination, subjectivity should be discouraged.

Criteria for evaluating the quality of programs must include as much factual data as possible, as well as sound external assessment. External assessment techniques should include the judgments of the college administration and peers from other institutions. The process by which this evaluation occurs is critical and cannot be overestimated. The ability to make qualitative distinctions among programs ultimately affects the future of academic institutions.

Conclusion

The issue is relatively simple: do we, in the long term, want institutions of quality that address our varied missions and respond to those values we hold dear, or can we satisfy ourselves with mediocrity? If we make decisions primarily to serve our colleagues rather than our students, the result is obvious. The public will grow increasingly intolerant of supporting expensive institutions that exist primarily to perpetuate their own interests. If quality and service are the hallmarks of our colleges and universities, the public will be willing to support our institutions at great sacrifice.

The easy course—the less controversial alternative of across-the-board reduction—is not the most advisable. Higher education is undergoing the most serious economic scrutiny of recent times. Will we rise to the occasion? Quality people beget quality people, and a quality program demands quality from its students. Faculty and staff in such programs rarely avoid or oppose review; review is more often challenged by those who have less confidence in their ability to meet high expectations. We have no choice but to make difficult, often painful, decisions about which programs stay and which programs go. Superficial collegiality is no substitute for quality. Selective program elimination is the most effective way to ensure quality in times of scarce resources.

Ronald J. Temple is president of Wayne County Community College, Michigan.

Decisions as to whether or not educational programs should be dropped or cut back should be based on data gathered from an effective program evaluation system.

Preserving and Enhancing Quality Through Effective Program Evaluation

Al Smith

In the two previous chapters, the authors have taken two very different positions with respect to enhancing the quality of curricula in the community college. Ronald J. Temple has argued that the best way to maintain quality is to eliminate weak programs or cut costs in other ways. John M. McGuire and Eldon Miller have suggested that in the long run such cutbacks may reduce the quality of the total educational program of two-year institutions. They maintain that comprehensiveness is an essential element in a high-quality program and that this comprehensiveness should be maintained as much as possible if community colleges are to succeed in the future.

The position taken in this chapter is that effective program evaluation can be used to identify weaknesses and ways to overcome these weaknesses in all the curricular offerings of a college. Program evaluation should be viewed as an ongoing improvement process, rather than as a one-time event to determine whether or not a specific department, degree program track, or course should be excluded from the curriculum. Effective program evaluation should eliminate most of the need to drop weaker programs. Under an effective program evaluation scheme, weaker programs will continually be improved or revised to meet the needs of new clientele. Only after extensive revisions have failed should programs be dropped from the comprehensive two-year college. The problem today is that too many faculty, department chairs, deans, and presidents are seeking a quick fix to their declining enrollments and increasing costs.

Because of the cyclical nature both of higher education programs and of the job market in our country, education programs should be dropped only after five to ten years of careful evaluation and revision. Once a program is dropped, it can take ten to twenty years to rebuild that program back into a strong, viable degree offering. A good example of this problem can be found in the area of the community college's transfer or liberal arts program. If colleges had dropped these programs in the 1970s because of declining enrollments, these same colleges would have had much more difficulty rebuilding these programs today to meet the renewed student interest in more academic, as opposed to occupational, education. The rebuilding process in general education and the liberal arts will be less costly in the 1980s and 1990s than it would have been had colleges drastically cut or eliminated faculty and programs in this area in the 1970s. The key to preserving and enhancing quality in community colleges in the next decade will be to develop program evaluation systems that will identify and correct program weaknesses as they occur. The key to success will be the development of general education, transfer, developmental, occupational, and community service programs that are continually being changed to meet the changing needs of our society.

State- and Campus-Level Evaluation

Why Evaluate? The unprecedented growth seen in community colleges during the 1960s and 1970s has ended and has given way to a national concern calling for a re-evaluation of priorities and a new commitment to program excellence (Study Group on the Conditions of Excellence in American Higher Education, 1984). There was little need for evaluation prior to the 1980s because of the rapid growth of two-year colleges. Now funding has become less predictable, and the dangers of accepting the status quo have become evident. The emphasis on quality programs is seen at the national, state, and local levels in funding formulas that reinforce an institution's academic performance, rather than relying solely on quantity or enrollment totals. A number of states, including Florida, have recently taken the initiative to implement formative program review procedures. These procedures are intended to support local and state decisions regarding additional resource allocations. Evaluation has been the missing essential ingredient in curriculum development since the beginning of the community college movement. All of higher education has neglected to stress this important ingredient in any successful program, whether in business and industry, government, or education. The question today is no longer one of why to evaluate, but rather of how to evaluate.

State-Level Evaluation in Florida. Florida provides a good example of how other states around the country can begin to improve the quality of their community college programs through statewide evaluation schemes. During 1982, the Division of Community Colleges and the Council of Instructional Affairs determined that a formal process was needed to review all degree and certificate programs in Florida's community colleges. The purpose of this process was to assist colleges and state level administrators in program planning efforts, to support budget appropriations, and to promote an emphasis on excellence. One of the state's goals was to have students who are attending Florida's colleges score in the top 25 percent on nationally administered tests at the end of five years.

In July 1983, the legislature assigned responsibility for the state-level program review to the State Board of Community Colleges. Twelve community colleges piloted and evaluated the preliminary evaluation program for the state. After piloting the program review model, four subcommittees were formed to address particular problem areas identified in the pilot study. An A.A. degree subcommittee, an occupational/vocational program subcommittee, a management information systems subcommittee, and a final implementation subcommittee were formed to develop the new program.

The state's model measures the following nine indicators of an academic program's effectiveness: (1) annual enrollment; (2) program success—total number of students completing the program, number of students completing the program and employed in the field or transferred to an upper-division school, and number of students leaving the program prior to completing all requirements; (3) full-time equivalents (FTEs); (4) cost of instruction per FTE; (5) equipment costs per FTE area; (6) student-to-faculty FTE ratio; (7) transfer GPA for A.A. program participants; (8) College Level Academic Skills Test (CLAST) scores for A.A. program participants; and (9) average licensure scores (Romanik, 1984, p. 7)

In addition to the above measures, specific criteria have been proposed for each of the above indicators. Each criterion was designed to provide a "flagging" mechanism, which helps locate programs that may need further review. The criteria provide either an expected range for an indicator or a value below or above which the indicator is flagged.

Florida's program review model will be continually changing until a workable design is reached. The fact remains, however, that the state review process is here to stay and that it is spreading to other states. This is a very positive trend for the improvement of the curriculum of two-year colleges, provided the colleges in each state participate in the development of their state plans, and provided each college develops its own local evaluation program.

Campus Program Evaluation Plans. The elimination of curriculum programs and the development of comprehensive, high-quality community college programs in the future will depend not so much on effective state evaluation plans, although they will help, as they will on effective, local-campus program evaluation schemes. Sound ongoing evaluation at this level will ensure the continuation of most academic programs. The position taken here is that most educational programs will continue to prosper and grow in an environment of continual feedback and correction. Such local evaluation schemes are being developed in many community colleges around the country. The argument here is that these will be the colleges that will avoid having to cut programs in the future. Instead of cutting programs or comprehensiveness, these colleges will contain programs that are constantly changing to meet the changing needs of their clientele and to serve the needs of new students.

In the next few paragraphs, the local-campus program evaluation plans of two community colleges are briefly described. The purpose of this review is to suggest some ways that colleges without a local evaluation plan can go about establishing such plans. The plans reviewed are for the Mitchell Wolfson New World Center Campus of Miami–Dade Community College and the Dallas County Community College District Occupational Education Plan.

Mitchell Wolfson New World Center Campus. The campus review model at this college involves a participatory review process whereby faculty and students directly and indirectly participate. In order to establish communication between the evaluators and those affected by the evaluation, the Academic Planning and Program Review Committee (APPR), composed of seven members representing six campus departments and divisions, was established. APPR has been given the responsibility of overseeing the evaluation activities, the selection of evaluation variables, the construction of evaluation instruments, and the setting of standards. The director of program evaluation and data management serves as the chair of this group. Since starting in February of 1984, the committee has finalized two program review strategies, the department audit and the academic program review. For the committee, evaluation represents a set of procedures for appraising an academic unit's merits, outcomes, and impact. Program evaluation is defined at this campus as the process of specifying, collecting, analyzing, and interpreting information about academic units in order to arrive at informed value judgments concerning continuation and modification. Note that this definition stresses continuation and modification of programs, rather than the discontinuance of programs.

The department audit report represents a formative evaluation strategy and is meant to be a routine monitoring of data that can identify potential change or problem areas in an academic department. The process is not intended to do more than indicate that a given department may need more detailed evaluation.

Six indicators are used in the audit process. These include two output measures (course retention rate and course success rate), three process measures (percent of enrollment projection, percent of productivity goal, and percent of expenditure projection), and one opinion measure (faculty evaluation of departmental operations). The audit is conducted each term, and audit indicators are traced on a standardized measuring scale, so that a single summary statistic will result for each indicator, each department, and each term. These index scores allow for intraindicator comparisons, therefore enabling each department chair to determine the six indicators on which the department performed best and which need the most work.

The program review model adopted by the campus represents a summative evaluation concerning particular academic programs offered at the Mitchell Wolfson New World Center Campus. Six indicators have been selected by APPR. The indicators include five output measures: percent of program completers employed; percent of program completers transferred; percent of A.A. degree students passing the CLAST and mid-CLAST; the percent of degree-seeking students awarded degrees; and upper-division GPA of graduates. There is also one process measure, annual enrollment. Performance on each of these six program review indicators will be traced in the same manner as those measured in the audit process. Additionally, the weighting of each indicator or measure according to campus and state priorities is also an intergral part of this program review process.

Both the review strategies outlined here represent only a portion of the emphasis that is being placed on preserving and enhancing quality at this campus in future academic years. It is this writer's strong belief that efforts such as these, which monitor and self-regulate quality on an ongoing basis, will greatly enhance program quality in the community college field in the future.

Dallas County Community College District Occupational Education Plan. The occupational education program evaluation system at Dallas County Community College District (DCCCD) is another good example of how program evaluation can be used to preserve and enhance quality in the two-year college (Dallas County Community College District, 1981). Here, the college has developed an evaluation format that is intended to be a minimum guide in evaluating all DCCCD occupational programs over a three-year cycle. In order for the evaluation results to be useful, every effort has been made to complete the program evaluation process during a twelve-month period, with evaluations beginning in the fall.

Because occupational program evaluation is basically a campus activity of DCCCD, the division chairpersons and the technical/occupational dean have had active roles in the entire process. The dean provides overall guidance and supervision of the process on campus. To assist campus personnel, the district staff has provided data on cost, enrollment, student interest, and follow-up.

The first step in the three-year cycle has been for the dean and other campus administrators to identify the programs to be evaluated each semester. Programs are identified at least one year in advance of the evaluation process; a program evaluation schedule for the whole college has been developed. Similar programs are evaluated during the same semester or year. For example, if three college campuses have an auto mechanics program, those programs are evaluated together during the same semester.

The college has found that it is helpful to have an occupational program evaluation committee on each campus for this process. The functions of that committee have included assisting the dean in making assignments and sharing the work load of collecting the appropriate data. The data collected have been categorized under five categories: program demand, student interest, instructional factors, graduate/completer performance, and cost factors. (Detailed descriptions of the types of data collected in each of these areas are not given here but can be obtained by writing to the college.) Once data collection and compilation have been completed, the dean invites the assistant director of occupational education (the general district coordinator/facilitator for the evaluation activity) to review the data, suggest further collection or analysis, and assist in the formulation of recommendations.

The division chairperson then develops a preliminary report, which is submitted to the dean, the vice-president of instruction, and the college president. The vice-president of instruction then convenes a program evaluation review meeting of all key persons involved or affected to discuss the preliminary review and to determine future action. Upon completion of the campus review, a final report is developed by the division chairperson and the dean. This report is then kept on campus, and a condensed version is submitted to the district director of occupational education for review and further action.

The key to success at Dallas County Community College District appears to be the emphasis on program evaluation and strategic planning. The college believes that the successful comprehensive community college, charged with the responsibility of meeting a broad spectrum of educational needs, must systematically evaluate its programs' relevancy and quality if it is to meet those needs.

A Curriculum Planning Model for the 1990s

A new curriculum planning model that has program evaluation as its central focus is needed in the two-year college field. This chapter has already shown how one state and two colleges are moving in the direction of establishing such a model. Two-year colleges cannot expect to achieve excellence without a curriculum planning model that requires continual program evaluation. Smith and Clements (1984) have proposed a curriculum planning model that stresses the importance of program evaluation and they make it central to the curriculum planning process. One of the major new approaches in this model is its emphasis on needs assessment as the starting point for all curriculum development; most curriculum planning models of the past and present start with the establishment of goals and objectives. Too often, this more traditional approach to curriculum development and evaluation has led to the creation of new courses or degree programs that are not based on community needs. For this reason, it is recommended that all curriculum improvement projects start with a needs assessment. The other major components of this newly proposed curriculum planning model are (1) developing college mission statements, (2) establishing program and course goals and objectives, (3) program evaluation, (4) developing program resources, (5) selecting appropriate learning activities, (6) implementing the system, and (7) evaluating the program in terms of intended and unintended outcomes.

The heart of this newly proposed curriculum planning model is program evaluation. Once a two-year college has completed a thorough needs assessment and established its mission, goals, and program objectives (the first three steps of the model), it should then consider conducting an evaluation of all existing programs over three-to-five years. This program evaluation should take place before any new courses or programs are added to a college's offerings or any old ones are deleted or revised.

Summary

There are no simple answers to solving the financial dilemmas of community colleges or to achieving excellence in the community college curriculum. Nevertheless, the two are integrally related. Even in an era of economic crisis, every curriculum decision should involve a careful program evaluation before courses or programs are added or deleted. A sound program evaluation process that involves the collection of both quantitative and qualitative data will go a long way toward the improvement of two-year college programs.

References

Dallas County Community College District. *Occupational Educational Program Evaluation: Format Guidelines.* Dallas: Dallas County Community College, 1981.
Romanik, D. *Preserving and Enhancing Quality Program Evaluation.* Miami: Miami–Dade Community College, 1984.
Smith, A. B., and Clements, C. *Meeting the Changing Needs: Undergraduate Curriculum and Instruction.* New York: Associated Faculty Press, 1984.
Study Group on the Condition of Excellence in American Higher Education. *Involvement In Learning: Realizing the Potential of American Higher Education.* Washington, D.C.: National Institute of Education, 1984.

Al Smith is professor of educational leadership and assistant director of the Institute of Higher Education at the University of Florida, Gainesville.

Part 4. Differential Salaries for Faculty

Salary disparities are antithetical to the realities and values of community colleges.

If You're So Smart, Why Aren't You Rich?

Phyllis Woloshin

"In today's fast-changing economy, there are new openings every day in high-paying jobs such as: Computer Geek; Drug Overload; Industrial Robot; Person Who Sells Staples to the Defense Department for What It Cost to Liberate France; Fugitive Financier; Vigilante; and Pip, whose responsibilities include standing behind Gladys Knight and going "Whoo-whoo" at exactly the right moment in the song "Midnight Train to Georgia." So, if anyone says there aren't enough well-paying jobs out there, there are. The problem is, who wants them?" (Barry, 1985, p. 37).

Whenever I told anybody my major was philosophy, the immediate response was, "What can you do with that?" Fresh out of graduate school in the mid-1950s, I started my job search. Most of the secretaries I spoke to laughed and offered a variation of "Are you kidding? Philosophers die in their jobs. If I were you, honey, I'd take up typing." Seventeen years, two more degrees, and three careers later, I found myself applying again for a job teaching philosophy. I have been teaching ever since. If I had stayed in auditing, my original major, I would probably be making two or three times as much money as I do now. My response to "Why didn't you?" is "Who wanted to?"

The assumption that money is the measure of personal and professional motivation is one of several underlying myths that arise the minute discussion

B. W. Dziech (Ed.), *Controversies and Decisions in Hard Economic Times*. New Directions for Community Colleges, no. 53. San Francisco: Jossey-Bass, March 1986.

of salary differentials among community college faculty begin. The one point upon which everyone agrees is that funding for our colleges is inadequate. The quickest way to deal with such a problem in a labor-intensive industry is to gear pay to market fluctuations and ignore the priorities on which higher education is founded. The problem with that solution is that it embraces too many myths and overlooks too many of the realities of higher education.

Problem 1: Salary differentials are unrealistic because they assume that people are motivated by money. Although salary differentials are part of the support system undergirding the work ethic, and although they exist in teaching just as they do across and among other professions, people still enter teaching as a profession. If not money, what is it that keeps people coming to colleges to learn about and teach subjects that have no immediate competitive value in the marketplace? If their earnings are limited by the marketplace, why do they continue to teach? The answer seems obvious: By and large, those who teach are people who like what they do and feel that what they do is important, even though they know they will not get rich doing it. They are people whose values are not solely monetary.

For many, "psychic" benefits help mitigate the monetary drawbacks of teaching. Teaching offers freedom and time flexibility, availability of an intellectual community, and, most important, the feeling that the work and one's contribution are important. In the long run, "psychic salary" may be the major attraction to teaching. What has always distinguished the faculties of higher education is their sense of vocation and their belief in the missions of their institutions. It is appropriate to talk about salaries in terms of dollars and cents, but we must also keep in mind these other considerations turn out to be as important as money.

The argument that salaries must be market-driven is an artificial one. It says that if you offer enough dollars to the computer specialist, he or she will come to teach at your institution. It neglects the issue of interest in the work itself. It says that the business or engineering major will be attracted to teaching if he or she is offered enough money. The monetary-reward argument disregards personal and private incentives in professions. It ignores the cultures of organizations and the individual differences in people's wants and desires; indeed, it ignores the very understanding of the human condition that the liberal arts foster and that most technologies were created to enhance.

Problem 2: Salary differentials are unrealistic because they assume high-demand disciplines remain constant over time. Those who argue in favor of market-driven pay for faculty assume that demand in an area will remain constant over time. The literature tells us otherwise. Alfred and Nash (1983) contend that the emerging problem of community colleges is the "need to retrain or revitalize faculty in career programs to improve the performance of the institution in relation to changing economic conditions, shifting labor market needs, and rapid advances in technology" (p. 3). They observe that community college programs will be in a "constant state of flux" (p. 4) for the rest of the decade, since there are changing patterns in student interest and "an increasingly common horizontal transition" (p. 4) in the jobs themselves. The issue here is this: If certain faculty members' disciplines were once in high demand, why are they no longer high priority? If we face years of "shifting labor market needs," can we afford to tie our economics to high salaries that may eventually be unjustified?

The assumption of the "steady state" ignores the realities of the world beyond the campus. Management guru Harlan Cleveland, dean of the Hubert Humphrey Institute of Public Affairs, believes that since the United States produces mainly information, management leadership calls for generalists, because it is no longer possible for any one person to know enough about all the technical aspects of things. Good leadership requires fundamental knowledge and empathy, and industry has recognized this for a long time (Ritter, 1985). One of the Big Eight multinational accounting firms has a policy of hiring 40 percent liberal arts graduates and 60 percent lawyers and accountants. Why not 100 percent professionally and vocationally trained people? The company's rationale is that liberal arts graduates are easier to train. They can learn the details of the profession quickly and in the long run are better able to handle people and change than those who are narrowly trained. If this is so, the high-demand faculty member may not be so indispensable as some contend.

Scientific information has quadrupled in the last twenty-five years. With that kind of expansion, how could anyone argue that current high-demand disciplines will remain constant? Most technologies gobble each other up within a year or two, and so the real question to ask ourselves is "What is the sticking power of, for example, data processing as compared to, for example, history of Western civilization?" When data processing becomes subsumed under a more complex technology, what will become of the high-salaried employees who were so urgently needed today?

Problem 3: Salary differentials are unrealisitc because they assume attitudes toward other disciplines and toward faculty are unaffected when one kind of teaching is more highly rewarded than another. The offer of greater compensation for one type of teaching over another implies that one type of learning and one type of professor are more highly valued than another. In some respects, this is the most serious issue of the market-driven salary concept. Salary differentials are dangerous because they corrode both the public and private status of currently low-demand subject areas; this in turn erodes an important "psychic" benefit of teaching. When entry-level salaries for those who wish to teach in low-demand fields reflect societal devaluation, the teaching profession becomes unattractive to the best and the brightest. When senior faculty find themselves and their services devalued, their temptation to flee the profession is increased.

In a recent article, Prokasky (1984) comments on the "costly consequences" of salary disparities: "One of the most obvious is poor faculty morale and, with it, the flight of the best faculty members to alternative occupations. That has been the case with many outstanding secondary-school teachers, and there is no reason to think that eroded salaries in institutions of higher education won't have the same effect" (p. 80).

Currently, of course, the second-class faculty are those in the humanities. Lower pay is a way of reminding the public that while what they do has a certain quaint intrinsic value, it really is not very applicable to today's fast-paced society. The implication is that these low-demand courses are rather like the Polish army, which, having no modern equipment, mounted horses in full regalia and, brandishing swords, rode out to meet the oncoming Nazi tanks.

But then again, history records just the opposite—impressive victories over the huge, efficient machinery of developed nations by little more than powerful, embedded belief systems. With all our advanced technologies and efficiency, we lost the Vietnam conflict; Christianity overcame Rome; Judaism survived not only the Babylonian and Egyptian dispersions but also the efficiency of the "final solution" of one of the most technologically well-educated cultures, Nazi Germany.

What these seemingly dissimilar outcomes of conflict tell us is that futile gestures from either the powerful or the seemingly powerless, while immediately satisfying, ultimately lead to annihilation. Our entrenched thinking about salaries and education is about to do us in. We must do more than gesture about faculty pay. The manner in which community colleges support education—from eager tooling of shops to higher salaries for work-oriented technologists—is merely a quick fix that will not solve the long-term financial problems of our institutions.

Indeed, the quick-fix approach may create even greater problems if it tempts us to forsake our original mission. As educators, we must remind ourselves of the basic values on which our institutions are founded. If general education is no longer a respected goal, if technocrats are really worth more than humanists, then we will in effect be rattling our swords in a grand gesture that is ultimately a futile one, for we will have lost our commitment to our own values.

Problem 4: Salary differentials are unrealistic because they assume teaching is like any other job. Salary disparities make the profession a trade rather than a vocation. The hidden message in the monetary-reward argument is that teaching is really not a profession, a calling, that all you need is trained, credentialed people in a high-demand field, coupled with people wanting to learn about it and willing to pay for it. The assumption is that education will magically happen when those who want to learn and those who have information are put in the same place at the same time. At best, this argument reflects our social attitudes toward teachers and teaching. There are those who believe that all we need is the right alchemical combination and we can automatically produce gold, that anyone can do it if you pay him or her enough. What evolves is a devaluation of teaching as a profession. The subject becomes more important than the learner or the teacher, and dollars are more important than both.

May (1980) reminds us: "The location of professional training within the university should not only nurture the professional as a critic and citizen but also cultivate him or her as a teacher. The professional needs to be more than a dispenser of technical services; he must accept his role with his clients and patients as instructor" (p.210).

Excellent teachers and excellent learning institutions have a vision of their tasks and purposes. They are committed to the value of what they do. This feeling of the worth of the endeavor is called the culture of an institution. If the culture of the institution has been lost, or if it devalues its sense of mission, then the institution itself will falter.

Conclusion

The private sector has had a significant impact on the academic world. We try to contain costs and to become cost-efficient; we talk about high-demand courses and salary differentials. In doing so, we forget that one of the most treasured characteristics of educational institutions has been their resistance to quick change (to put it another way, their respect for tradition). That resistance has given us stability in a rapidly changing world where knowledge itself has often become dangerous.

To survive, community colleges must rely on reality, rather than on assumptions. Our reality is that we have a need to retool for the age of technology and to train people to live and work in that age and that we have an equally important need to educate for life. In earlier times the two went hand in hand. Sons followed their fathers' trades and professions, and daughters replicated their mothers' lives. While we can wax nostalgic about the good old days, they are gone and will not return. Our fathers are no longer shepherds, and our mothers live long beyond the childbearing years. Our lives make more demands on us than learning to survive in our immediate environments.

We live in a global village, but our universities and colleges reflect separation instead of integration of thought and action. To discuss diversity in salary is an inevitable consequence of the "intellectual curtain separating faculties of science and faculties of arts" (Ashby, 1958, p. 74). If the university is to adapt itself fully to scientific revolution, it will have to eliminate from its machinery of government anything that aggravates this artificial distinction between groups of subjects.

History records the names of playwrights, sculptors, philosophers, historians, and orators. If I were to say the name Leonardo da Vinci, one probably would think of the *Last Supper* painted on a refectory wall, not of a helicopter; and if I were to say the name Michelangelo, one probably would think of the statue of David standing in a plaza in Florence, Italy, not of the architectural feat of the duomo in Rome. These men were valued not for their marketability but for their ability to capture the hearts and minds of the people who knew their work. Without someone supporting their vision, we probably would not have had the benefit of their brilliance. If there were no teachers to pass this heritage down to us, we would be bereft of culture and civilization. There is a distinct danger to us all if we minimize the importance of the work of low-demand, high-tradition subject matters. The point is that they never lose their vitality or their value.

Athletes make more money than I will ever see in a lifetime of teaching. So do gamblers, auto racers, oil barons, television stars, and physicians. I am none of those things, nor, if I had the same skills and were the same person I am now, would I want to be.

References

Alfred, R., and Nash, N. "Faculty Retraining, A Strategic Response to Changing Resources and Technology." *Community College Review*, 1983, *11* (2), 3-8.
Ashby, E. *Technology and the Academics.* London: Macmillan, 1958.
Barry, D. "Notes on Western Civilization." *Chicago Tribune Magazine*, June 2, 1985, p. 37.
May, W. "Professional Ethics: Setting, Terrain, and Teacher." In D. Callahan and S. Bok (eds.), *Ethics Teaching in Higher Education.* New York: Plenum, 1980.
Prokasky, W. "The Dilemma Colleges Face on Pay Scales." *Chronicle of Higher Education*, October 10, 1984, p. 80.
Ritter, L. *New York Times Book Review*, Sept. 8, 1985, p. 25.

Phyllis Woloshin is professor of philosophy at Oakton Community College, Illinois.

The principle of pay for top market value is not a theory but a necessity, and it can work effectively if the institution and its personnel are willing to recognize individual circumstances and to work together to develop a more coherent salary policy.

Competing with the Marketplace: The Need to Pay Some Faculty More

Thomas E. Wagner

Traditional approaches to determining college faculty salaries are no longer viable. In an era of limited financial resources, rapid technological advancement, and increased competition with industry and business, it is time for college faculty and administrators to re-examine outdated approaches to faculty pay and consider ways of meeting the demands of the future.

With the exception of arguments about limited space on campus, faculty salaries are probably the most emotional issue an academic administrator has to face. The salary policies at most institutions were developed by trial and error over time and are thus the result of past traditions, rather than of informed policy decisions. On too many campuses, faculty salary policies were not determined by those currently responsible for institutional policy, but rather by persons who have long since been forgotten. The irony is that contemporary academicians will spend hours justifying an existing salary policy, which they did not design and which creates enormous problems, but they will give very little consideration to the possibility of developing a new and more equitable and rational approach to remuneration of faculty.

If they did so, they would need to recognize that a number of factors are currently relevant to determining faculty pay. These include years of service, academic rank, teaching ability, research and scholarship, community and institutional service, the type and geographical location of the institution, and the market value of the professor's discipline (Tuckman, 1976). They would also be forced to admit that, of these, the latter demands far more serious consideration than it has been accorded previously. However painful the prospect, community college leaders must recognize that marketability of faculty is a concept they can no longer ignore.

The Urgent Need for Differential Funding

Sojka (1985, p. 12) observes, "The type of college or university and its perceived mission must . . . be considered with regard to the problem of coping with compensation for faculty in high-demand areas. . . . A clear understanding of the institution's ultimate goals is needed by administrators, faculty members, and trustees who must grapple with this perplexing problem, for decisions regarding compensation, possibly more than any other single factor, determine the composition, morale, and performance of the faculty." More than any other higher education institution, the community college defines its mission in terms of the here and now, the immediate needs of the communities it serves. For this reason, it is compelled to face the dilemma of differential compensation with urgency and decisiveness.

By and large, the differences in the salary policies from campus to campus result from the amount of discretion exercised in setting the salary of an individual faculty member (Simpson, 1981, p. 220). Compensation policies can be categorized from the most flexible to the most automatic. In the first and most flexible category are those institutions where administrators and faculty members hold separate negotiations on salary and each individual is treated according to circumstances. A second method is that of informal negotiations, with guidelines; for example, there may be minimum and maximum salaries at each rank. The third category is more structured; there is a minimum salary, and then there are basic steps through which a person moves as a result of discretionary decisions. A fourth, more structured system is one where there are minimum salary rates by rank, with automatic salary steps within ranks; advancement in rank may require a discretionary decision based on qualitative factors. Finally, there is the most structured salary policy, that in which people enter at the bottom of the salary schedule and move up automatically upon completion of preset requirements, such as years of service or attainment of academic degrees.

Higher education, and two-year colleges in particular, are facing financial limitations that force re-examination of salary policies and require adjustment of these policies so that the institutions can continue to provide quality education. Twenty years ago it was possible to offer most faculty similar pay rates, regardless of discipline, but the realities of the present make such simplicity impracticable.

In a recent study of salary differences across disciplines, Hansen (1985, p. 6) examines variations in faculty compensation over a period from 1976–77 to 1984-85. While he does not analyze the community college in particular, his data are relevant because the high-demand disciplines he discusses are generally offered in related forms in two-year colleges. Most people, for example, are aware that faculty in the law, engineering, business, and computer fields typically receive higher pay than faculty in other disciplines, particularly the humanities and social sciences. The differences between salaries by discipline are very similar, both for full professors and for newly hired junior faculty members, and Hansen's study clearly reveals that there are greater differences in the salary differentials of the disciplines in 1984-85 than in 1976-77.

Hansen believes there are several reasons for the wider range of salary differentials in the 1980s. First, the overall decline in average real faculty salaries led to a widening of the gap between salaries in higher education and those in the private sector. This erosion in faculty salaries led to the recruitment by industry and business of large numbers of faculty in high-demand disciplines. Colleges countered by offering higher salaries to new faculty and by raising the salaries of current faculty. Second, the demand by business and industry for people with training in engineering, computer sciences, and business expanded more rapidly than the demand for all private-sector personnel as a whole. Students, quick to sense trends in the job market, reacted quickly, with the result that enrollment in high-technology and business fields increased rapidly. These combined forces increased the demand for faculty members in these disciplines. Thus, forces in the private sector drove up salaries for faculty in certain fields, especially business, engineering and computer sciences. This high demand for faculty in certain disciplines creates two problems for colleges. First is the need to pay higher salaries to new faculty in these specialty areas. A second and equally perplexing problem is the salary compression between senior and newly employed faculty.

In the 1980s, we have come to realize that most faculty will probably remain where they are for quite some time. It is not possible, as in the past, for most academicians to move to new positions. Greater turnover in the past meant that institutions had more flexibility within salary lines to manipulate pay, but today people are staying on campuses longer, and their salaries are increasing. This means that salary costs are, in one sense, beyond the control of the institution. Even early retirement has not had a great impact on the growing cost of fixed-salary populations. Inflation, although it has abated somewhat, is another unattractive reality with which colleges must live. A third problem is that higher education has become increasingly labor-intensive. In most instances, approximately 80 to 90 percent of an institution's budget is committed to paying its personnel. This leaves little or no room for negotiating salaries with individuals. Finally, although many are not willing to recognize or admit the fact, salaries in academe are tied closely to the job market. All these influences contribute to the complexity of the economic situation on college campuses. Viewed collectively, they demonstrate the compelling need for more realistic ways to compensate faculty.

Faculty in certain disciplines, such as business, high-technology areas, and computer science, are demanding and receiving higher salaries ("Average Faculty Salaries. . . . ," 1985, p. 30). In order to hire an accounting professor, for example, an institution must pay more than for an English or a history professor. Even when accountants or computer scientists are paid more, salaries in higher education are still substantially below the job market in the business community. Many faculty in high-demand disciplines could probably earn half again or twice their salaries if they worked in industry or business.

Forces Operating Against Differential Funding

Despite the facts, the pressure on most campuses is for equalization of faculty salaries, but such equality will not help to meet the demands of a complex situation. Faculty and administrators talk about teaching and public and institutional service as important factors in determining remuneration, but the truth is that excellent teaching and service do not make a faculty member more salable. If one is a good teacher, involved in public or campus service, that fact is recognized locally. However, national reputations are seldom based on these considerations. In the national job market, people are paid for their scholarly reputations or for the market value of their skills. In other words, they are paid for their value to their disciplines and for the discipline's value to the institution.

Most colleges cannot afford to insist on a tightly structured salary system, with everyone paid at the same rate. Those that do will have great difficulty recruiting faculty in high-demand disciplines. An institution that wants a high-quality engineering technology program must employ people who are competitive in the market; to do that, it must pay them what they can earn in the market. This does not mean that the college must meet exactly the salary an individual would earn in industry. There are intrinsic values attached to working on a campus. Faculty members have more discretionary time and more freedom than colleagues in industry. Further, faculty members may be able to supplement academic salary with pay from consulting work or summer and evening teaching. The institution can stress these unusual benefits for working in higher education, but it must also be able to establish salary levels that will allow it to compete for high-technology personnel.

The debate on a campus over using market factors based on discipline in determining faculty salaries can be acrimonious and demoralizing. It is an issue that can quickly destroy faculty collegiality if some faculty perceive themselves in either a "have" or "have not" situation because of their disciplines. Those who oppose market factors being used in determining faculty salaries raise several objections. Foremost is the view that all faculty members, regardless of discipline, are ultimately the same; that is, they teach students, engage in professional activities, and provide service to the institution and community. Therefore, they contend, compensation levels should be similar for all persons of similar rank, without consideration for discipline. Some will concede that individual differences in compensation might be based on such factors as rank or the quality of performance of one's assigned duties. These same persons also argue that college administrators and faculty must guard against overreacting to temporary job market fluctuations, that we must avoid the "quick pay fix" in response to higher education's competition with business and industry. They believe that it is unrealistic to assume that community and two-year colleges can seriously compete financially with industry for the talents of high-technology graduates.

The latter argument is particularly weak. It is possible for community colleges to compete for the most qualified faculty. There are many intrinsic benefits to working in an institution of higher education. Many individuals will sacrifice higher pay because of their love of teaching. Others will exchange higher salaries for freedom from constraint and fewer time demands. The point is that few private-sector organizations can compete with the opportunities higher education can provide for flexibility of work schedules, professional autonomy, job security, and creative and varied career endeavors.

Another argument against market-based pay is that the current situation is only one swing of the supply-and-demand cycle. Many hold that within a short period of time, supply will catch up with demand, and then institutions will have too many highly paid faculty members in certain disciplines. Historical data do not support this argument. Hansen's (1985) study, cited earlier, indicates that the highly paid, high-demand disciplines today are the same as ten years ago. Further study would show that faculty in these disciplines were paid more than other faculty even twenty years ago. Although the salary gap between the higher-paid and lower-paid disciplines has widened, the disciplines are basically the same (Katz, 1973, p. 474).

Finally, those opposed to salary based on the market value of the discipline fall back on the argument that differential pay violates the intrinsic values of higher education; that is, if we pay some people more than others simply on the basis of the demand for their skills in our society, we are abandoning our commitment to educating the whole person. The argument here is that when we abandon that commitment, we are saying to the community that we value the person who understands the intricacies of computers more than we value people who have devoted their lives to exploring the intricacies of the human mind or the works of man. Such is not the case, for it does not follow that if we pay someone on the basis of his or her value in the job market, we must change our views about what is needed to be an educated person. What it does say is that we recognize the realities of society and do not live in ivory towers.

The Need for Appropriate Action

These and other arguments against the use of market factors for determining faculty salaries can be heard on most campuses, but an institution's refusal to consider job market conditions can result in its inability to provide quality instruction to its students. What is needed is for each institution to study its salary policies carefully. Colleges' compensation procedures must be designed with full consideration for institutional circumstances and histories. The type of college, the community it serves, and its perceived mission are among the factors that must be considered in establishing a salary policy. The procedure must be acceptable to and understood by both faculty and administration. There must be specific reasons, understood by all, for paying people the salaries they receive.

In a period of limited resources, it is critical that personnel understand the financial realities with which their institutions must cope. The principle of pay for top market value is not a theory but a necessity, and it can work effectively if the institution and its personnel are willing to recognize individual circumstances and to work together to develop a more coherent salary policy. The very survival of many community colleges in the immediate future will depend not only on their ability to meet the demands of the market place but also on whether they can do so with the courage and honesty necessary to survive in a complex society. We must be able to meet our commitments, even when doing so requires that we make difficult and unpopular decisions.

References

"Average Faculty Salaries by Rank in Selected Fields." *Chronicle of Higher Education*, May 9, 1985, p. 30.
Hansen, L. W. "Salary Differences Across Disciplines." *Academe*, 1985, *71* (4), 6-7.
Katz, D. A. "Faculty Salaries, Promotions, and Productivity at a Large University." *The American Economic Review*, 1973, *63* (3), 469-477.
Simpson, W. P. "Faculty Salary Structure for a College or University." *Journal of Higher Education*, 1981, *10*, 219-236.
Sojka, G. A., "Balancing Academic Performance and Market Conditions." *Academe*, 1985, *71* (4), 11-13.
Tuckman, H. P. *Publication, Teaching, and the Academic Reward Structure.* Lexington, Mass.: D. C. Heath, 1976.

Thomas E. Wagner is vice-provost at the University of Cincinnati.

Economic pressures have resulted in institutions' paying some faculty more than others. Many are concerned about the growing gap in pay between humanists and social scientists, as opposed to faculty with high open-market value.

New Approaches to Faculty Compensation

James L. Wattenbarger

There is an obvious disagreement when discussions of salary levels begin. When such discussions continue and a variety of methods that could be used as bases for increasing salaries are brought into the picture, the disagreements not only sharpen but often become more strident. The peak of disagreement usually comes about when differentials related to discipline or to market value are recommended in order to increase the salaries for some, but not all, faculty. More recently, the term *comparable worth* has extended the basis for disagreement into another dimension. In such discussions, it has become well known that almost everyone can command a better salary in business-related or industry-related jobs than in teaching. In fact, some faculty have been known to use this alternative as a threat. Even the comic strip *Doonesbury* has a strip showing the professor of Latin threatening President King with his resignation, so that he can go to work in industry, unless his conditions for staying in the academic world are met forthwith. President King, I believe, was not impressed.

There is great fear, however, that the brightest and the best will go to other positions unless the salary schedule is modified to accommodate the market value of the professional discipline. We all tend to react to these problems in ways that reflect our personal situations and even our biases.

The chief executive officer of a community college will be concerned about budgets, salary schedules, union contracts, faculty morale, interdepartmental relationships, and auditors, to mention only a few of the worries that predominate during waking hours.

Faculty members will react most often in terms of their own situations. Those whose knowledge and personal skills enable them to view themselves as having potential value, and therefore marketability, in other positions will naturally want to take full advantage of those benefits. Those who teach in areas that do not readily appear to be marketable may have some difficulty accepting a market-value basis for salary.

Community college students may not react to this question at all. Their concern is to study with a good teacher who is capable, concerned, and fair; they are not ordinarily very much concerned about the individual teacher's reputation, marketability, or contributions outside the classroom.

The general public, as represented by the board of trustees, will seek stability, quality in instruction, and operations within the budget framework. Board members in general are not too concerned with the comparative marketability of individual faculty except in comparison with other educational institutions. Business and industry personnel raids are seldom anticipated and little feared.

Herzberg (1968) has conducted a series of studies that indicate that money is not a motivator but is a hygiene factor: Good salaries are necessary; higher salaries may make one feel better but are not a motivating factor in job performance. More important to a faculty member is a feeling of being necessary, worthwhile, and recognized as a contributor to the students.

There is no doubt that salary differentials exist both within a single institution and between institutions. Within a single institution, these differentials may be based on a number of factors, all of which have been built into the salary schedule. These usually are length of service and level of preparation, and sometimes merit may be considered.

Community colleges in many instances began operation as parts of public school systems. They inherited salary schedules that are fairly rigid. Laws often require single salary schedules, and auditors often track an individual's salary by using only the legal factors to determine it. A criterion is that anyone with the same basic data should be able to arrive at the same figure.

When the differentials are permitted, they must be based on identifiable factors that can be traced. The flexibility that is often characteristic of private colleges, or even that permitted in public senior colleges and universities, is not legally permitted in many public school systems and in community college districts. In other words, there is no legal basis for providing for market value in developing a salary schedule in many community college districts.

Developing Salary Schedules

What should be considered, then, in developing salary schedules for community colleges? One might well take two very different approaches to answer this question. The first approach should describe the situation when there is only one standard common salary schedule permitted; the second should describe a situation where more flexibility is possible.

In the first instance, the traditional basic salary schedule is developed around the level of educational preparation of an individual and the years of service. These two variables determine the location of an individual's salary on the schedule. These may be designated increments available for special assignments, such as department chair; special committee assignments; a student activity assignment, such as sponsor of a club; an athletic coaching assignment; or some other well-defined responsibility that is above and beyond the usual faculty load.

A base salary schedule is then developed, with steps or increments displayed on a scale. By moving down the years-of-service column to the row for appropriate educational level, one can find the specific salary for a specific individual. There may be different tables for the various faculty ranks, if such ranking is used.

The problems are solved when the scale tables are constructed. Institutional pay objectives can be built into the tables. For example, if a college wishes to recruit top-level new faculty, the beginning salary may be set relatively high and then balanced with no recognition (salary increase) after a determined year. If the college wishes to encourage faculty stability, the annual increases built in after a determined year may be large and consistent through another determined year.

For administrative salaries, a position classification system is needed, with an increment designated for each position number that is related to the level and type of responsibility associated with the position. These increments may be added to the base schedule used for total faculty, or a separate salary schedule may be developed that is unrelated to the basic one.

The second approach may be very similar to the first, with the exception that an additional amount of money is made available and awarded for merit. The determination of who receives a part of this merit award and who does not may be made in a number of ways. Recognition of the number and quality of publications is usually one criterion. Others that may be included are community contributions, students' evaluations of teaching effectiveness, quality of counseling and advising, research grants received, consultancies carried out, speeches made, service performed on committees, and special recognitions received. All of these require someone's judgment and involve measurements that are largely qualitative, as well as quantitative. The result may not be independently computed by all who examine the evidence. In other words, these levels are not always so easily audited.

It would also be possible to develop a ratio representing market value—a way of relating one discipline to another—that could be used to identify an increment to be added for that purpose as well. This second approach provides the flexibility that is usually missing in community college salary schedules and is used more often in four-year colleges and universities than in community colleges.

Salary Administration

Given the problems inherent in establishing satisfactory salary policies, the administrator working with the faculty has some very specific responsibilities in salary administration. He or she must be certain that a faculty remuneration system accomplishes certain goals:

1. It must be based on a comprehensive pay plan that is made up of several elements. These include a clear statement of the institution's pay objectives; a well-understood method for identifying, analyzing, and evaluating positions; a position classification schedule; a position evaluation plan; and a method for placing individuals in a proper category for pay.

2. It should assign clear administrative responsibilities for locating individuals on the pay schedule in accord with stated policy, conducting the annual evaluation procedures, conducting the salary survey for comparative data, supervising the implementation of the salaries within the pay plan, and maintaining the records.

3. It should provide for continued evaluation, updating, and the development of new policies, as needed.

The procedures for arriving at these policy statements should be based on wide participation within the college governance structure. The president and designated administrative personnel are responsible for providing leadership, with approved technical help, as needed. The basic point is to develop a policy for college pay objectives. What are the purposes that this community college expects to accomplish through the pay policy? Some questions that may be asked are the following:

1. Should the pay policy encourage stability in the faculty?
2. Should the pay policy encourage the employment of those who hold the doctorate?
3. Should the college encourage beginning employment of experienced faculty?
4. Should the college recognize market value of selected disciplines?
5. Should the college provide for evaluation of teaching performance?
6. Should the college develop criteria for merit, to be included in salary allocation? If so, what should these be?
7. Should the pay plan encourage faculty to provide a variety of community services?
8. Should the pay plan encourage improvement of teaching effectiveness?
9. Should the pay plan encourage faculty to publish articles, books, and monographs?
10. Should the pay plan encourage faculty to provide consultant services to the community?
11. Should the pay plan be based on evaluation procedures?
12. Should the pay plan encourage implementation of the philosophical values of the community college?

Essential Considerations

At the heart of the controversy over faculty pay are these fundamental questions about the purpose and commitments of community colleges. Amidst all the verbiage over market value and salary differentials, it is easy—and dangerous—to lose sight of these essential considerations. The most pragmatic of higher education institutions—the community college—can, if it chooses, discover equitable and satisfactory means of dealing with this latest financial adversity. What it cannot afford to do is allow the debate over faculty pay to obscure its mission or destroy the collegiality so vital to fulfilling that mission.

References

Herzberg, F. W. "One More Time: How Do You Motivate Employees?" *Harvard Business Review*, 1968, *46* (3), 82-91.

James L. Wattenbarger is director of the Institute of Higher Education, University of Florida, Gainesville.

Part 5. Further Sources of Information

*This chapter provides further sources of information on
controversial issues facing community college decision makers.*

Sources and Information: Decision Making in Hard Economic Times

Jim Palmer

Previous chapters of this sourcebook articulate divergent arguments surrounding four issues: (1) the increased use of part-time faculty, (2) the limitation of open-door admissions policies, (3) retrenchment and its effects on program quality, and (4) differential salaries for faculty. This concluding chapter draws on a review of the materials indexed in ERIC's *Resources in Education* and *Current Index to Journals in Education* to examine what other authors have had to say about these areas of concern.

Part-Time Faculty

Part-time faculty present community college administrators with a host of advantages. Hammons (1981) notes that part-timers provide considerable cost savings, bring business and technical expertise to the faculty, and allow administrators to try new programs without making long-term commitments to new, full-time faculty. He also points out that college relations with the community are improved when local citizens are hired as part-time instructors and that part-timers improve program flexibility. Eliason (1980) stresses the flexibility issue, arguing that part-time faculty, hired on a short-term or ad hoc basis, facilitate institutional responsiveness to changing educational needs. "The adult who turns to the two-year college . . . ," she maintains, "needs instant service—community colleges must be ready to provide work skills to match the changing requirements of the job market. A static faculty cannot provide this" (p. 9).

Yet most writers agree that the problems posed by part-timers are equally numerous and too often ignored. Hammons (1981) catalogues several administrative problems posed by part-timers: the growing proportion of nonteaching tasks (such as student advising) that must be borne by full-time faculty; the limited contacts adjunct staff have with full-timers and the concomitant alienation of part-time faculty from the college community; and growing demands for pro rata pay rates and for other privileges and benefits that are normally accorded full-time faculty. Hammons also notes that increases in the ranks of part-timers have not always been met with requisite attention to their supervision, evaluation, and professional development. Clearly, part-time faculty have often been hired without regard to the administrative tasks that need to be undertaken to ensure the integration of adjunct staff into the college community and to assess their continued instructional effectiveness.

Many critics contend further that part-timers are part of an abused secondary labor market within academe. Fryer (1977) notes the growing number of "permanent" part-time faculty, those who are hired year after year on a part-time basis, without the benefits and privileges accorded to full-time employees. Pollock and Breuder (1982) focus on the problems faced by these struggling instructors: unequal pay in relation to full-timers, denial of privileges and benefits, limited participation in governance and curriculum matters, low morale, and lack of commitment to the college. The end result, some maintain, is lowered institutional quality. Marsh and Lamb (1975) argue that by employing large numbers of temporary instructors, colleges "institutionalize second-class professionalism by promoting minimal commitment" (p. 17). Guthrie-Morse (1979) concurs: "Can an institution that features 56 percent part-time versus 44 percent full-time instructional employees survive in its present form? The 'community' will no longer imply a group of educators committed to the attainment of institutional goals and objectives, but rather will suggest a loose association of individuals who have major commitments to other jobs" (p. 17).

Do part-timers actually lower instructional quality? Research findings are mixed. Cruise, Furst, and Klimes (1980) report that no significant differences were found between part-timers and full-timers who were compared on the basis of self-evaluations, student evaluations, and administrator evaluations. In a similar study, Willett (1980) was unable to find significant differences between full-time and part-time staff in terms of student ratings, class retention, and subsequent student achievement in advance courses. In a national study, however, Friedlander (1979) found significant differences in the teaching experiences and practices of adjunct and full-time staff. Part-timers had less teaching experience, imposed less stringent reading requirements on students, utilized a smaller variety of instructional materials, made use of fewer out-of-class activities, and were less likely to take part in professional activities. Turgeon (1983) likewise found that full-time faculty at Corning Community College (New York) were older, more experienced, and had attained higher levels of formal education. Lolley (1980), in contrast, found that part-timers and full-timers at Tarrant County Community College (Texas) were quite similar in terms of use and knowledge of instructional techniques and media. The quality of part-time faculty, then, probably varies from institution to institution and depends, of course, on which quality measures are used. A more detailed analysis of this research and the literature on this issue is provided by Boggs (1984).

Despite criticisms in the literature, however, most college practitioners would probably agree with Hammons (1981) that part-timers will continue to be extensively used—the benefits they bring to the college (especially in terms of financial savings) are just too compelling. Rather than dropping the practice of hiring instructors on a part-time basis, many college leaders have initiated staff-development programs that are designed to integrate adjunct staff into the college community and to ensure their instructional effectiveness. Descriptions of these staff-development efforts are provided in numerous ERIC documents, including Parsons (1980), Winter, Fadale, and Anderson (1981), Peterson (1982), Elioff (1983), McCright (1983), Jones (1984), Phillips (1984), and Pedras (1985). While these development efforts are presented as sincere attempts to ameliorate the position of part-timers, some authors question the motivation behind these programs. Kekke (1984), for example, maintains that "it is possible that guilt, not genuine understanding of teaching, drives these attempts at development" (p. 9). She argues further that full-time careers must become available if community colleges are to attract the "best and brightest" of the nation's graduate schools (p. 11).

The Controversy of the Open Door

Another issue stirring debate among two-year college professionals is the question of open admissions and their effect on quality. Koltai and Wolf (1984) remind us that the question of access has been one of fluctuating emphasis throughout the history of two-year colleges and that "we now appear to be more concerned about quality" (p. 43). Hyde (1982) echoes these concerns, noting that "the attention given to promoting higher education opportunities is now waning" (p. 1). Questions concerning access, he maintains, are currently "secondary to concerns of quality, basic skills, student and faculty competence, budgetary practices, cost attainment, and accountability" (p. 1).

The literature on this issue, however, by no means signals an end to the open door. Henderson (1982) notes that "current opposition to the open-door philosophy is indirect in nature and focuses on the providing of quality education and the saving of money to taxpayers rather than opposition to the open door itself" (p. 30). Rather than calling for an end to open-admissions policies, writers have called for an improvement in the remedial and counseling services that are designed to help underprepared and nontraditional students succeed. Richardson (1983a) notes that many students who want to enroll in highly subscribed vocational programs never make it through the remedial and other introductory courses that are designed to make students eligible for program admission. He calls for more efficient placement and testing, for an analysis of the competencies needed to succeed in each program offered, and for counseling that will provide students with realistic information on their chances for program admission. Other authors, including Mirabeau (1977), Roueche (1981-82), and Roueche, Baker, and Roueche (1985), stress the need for improved teaching as a means of ensuring the success of students entering the open door. These writers call for instructional innovation and reform, such as interdisciplinary courses, the development of programs that will allow students to progress at their own pace, and the implementation of rigorous literacy instruction throughout the curriculum.

The current emphasis on quality over access, then, has resulted in a reform movement that is designed to improve students' chances of success, rather than to deny access. This reform movement is nowhere more evident than at Miami-Dade Community College (Florida). Between 1978 and 1983 the college undertook a comprehensive reform of its educational program that allowed the continuation of the open door while at the same time strengthening expectations and increasing the educational achievement of its graduates. The reform included the reinstatement of a placement testing program, the establishment of standards of academic progress to monitor student performance and control credit load, and the implementation of student information systems to provide individualized feedback on midterm academic performance and progress toward meeting graduation requirements (McCabe, 1983). Elements of this institutional reform are also described by Kelly and Anandam (1979), Anandam and others (1979), Lukenbill and McCabe (1978), and Harper and others (1981). Studies of the impacts of these reforms are provided by Losak (1983) and by Losak and Morris (1983a, 1983b). McCabe (1983) reports that the college experienced a sharp decline in graduation and re-enrollment rates after the reforms were implemented, but that these rates have since fully recovered.

Numerous authors have described other educational innovations and reforms that are designed to ensure the academic success of students entering through the open door. Most of these innovations center around student assessment and placement (Hartman, 1981; Ramey, 1981; Rivera, 1981; Beavers, 1983; Haase and Caffrey, 1983; Forstall, 1984; Friedlander, 1984; Haase and Caffrey, 1984; Hector, 1984; Neault, 1984; Rasor and Powell, 1984; Rounds, 1984; and Rounds and Andersen, 1984). Other writers have focused on (1) special programs for high-risk students (Henard and Adelman, 1982; Miller, 1982; Chausow and Barshis, 1983; and Davis and Luvaas-Briggs, 1983); (2) the use of computers to improve academic advising (Prince George's Community College, 1983; Donohue, 1984); and (3) interdisciplinary studies (Conkright, 1982; Harris, 1984; Landsburg and Witt, 1984; and Starks, 1984). The current emphasis on quality has clearly led to a re-emphasis of the teaching focus of the two-year college. Most of today's writers agree with Cohen (1975): "Open the door of admissions, but stop the strident advertising until some genuine alternatives in curriculum and instruction have been tested and installed so that people with different orientations can still benefit" (p. 51).

A by-product of this reform movement, however, is the growing conviction on the part of many college leaders that some students will simply not succeed. McCabe (1981) calls on colleges to recognize the point at which the student is not going to succeed and at which further public investment is not justified. Richardson (1983b) posits that "some may have to fail or even be excluded if higher education is to remain an avenue for social mobility for the academically underprepared" (p. 50). Further research is needed to determine just how far pedagogical innovation and reform can improve the educational success of the great variety of nontraditional students served by open-door community colleges.

Retrenchment and Quality

These calls for pedagogical reforms, however, come at a time when stable or reduced budgets threaten the comprehensive curriculum and the community college commitment to nontraditional programming. The California Postsecondary Education Commission (1983b) reports that reduced community college funding has diminished institutional responsiveness; students are offered a smaller variety of courses, especially in the areas of high technology and sophomore-level transfer courses. This diminished responsiveness is especially threatening, however, to nontraditional students. Hyde (1982) asserts that the "altruistic wave that supported the proliferation of colleges and special programs to assist disadvantaged individuals in the 1960s and 1970s is receding" (p. 124). Matson (1978) notes that student personnel services—so badly needed by nontraditional students—are often threatened in times of retrenchment. Rippey and Roueche (1977) maintain that as funding is decreased, "nontraditional students . . . will be the first to go." The prescription for retrenchment, Rippey and Roueche maintain, will be "deny access to none; just stop recruiting nontraditional students" (p. 57). The authors conclude that this ought to please the faculty, administrators, and legislators who "never wanted tax monies spent on those who 'shouldn't be in college anyhow'" (p. 57).

Budget cuts have been especially threatening to the community services curriculum. Although Zoglin (1982) argues that reduced funding should result in a de-emphasis of the transfer function (where alternative opportunities exist) and an expansion of community education programs, other writers point to a different scenario. Ireland and Feuers-Jones (1980) note that tax limitation measures in California have had a particularly deleterious effect on community services; after Proposition 13, self-supporting community services programs survived, while whole programs for seniors and the disadvantaged were cut. Reports describing retrenchment outcomes at individual institutions confirm that the de-emphasis on community services is not localized in California. Nichols and Stuart (1983) examine how Oakland Community College (Michigan) de-emphasized community services in response to fiscal exigencies. Keyser and Gonzales (1984) note that in an effort to develop a contingency plan for reduced funding, an ad hoc committee at Linn-Benton Community College (Oregon) prioritized community services last, after (respectively) vocational programs, lower-division transfer programs, and developmental programs. The literature indicates, then, that budget reductions have forced colleges to retreat to their original missions of credit programming in transfer and vocational areas. While the community services function has not been abandoned, it is certainly threatened. Casey (1982) summarizes the problem: "If there is a Dunkirk, I fear there will be no place to which we can retreat—unless it is to pure technical, noncollegiate institutions, or the traditional 'junior' colleges of the past" (p. 15).

In making curricular priorities, administrators are torn between the desirability of avoiding personnel layoffs and the need to eliminate low-priority programs. White (1978) argues that reductions in force should be a management tool of last resort, to be applied only after the termination of nontenured staff, the discontinuance of sections vacated by absent faculty, or the bare-bones reduction of the operating budget. Sussman (1978) disagrees, arguing that "the impulse to 'do the right thing' for faculty and staff . . . will have to be tempered by a long-term view of the most effective distribution of available resources to achieve the goals of the institution" (p. 41). Staff may also have to be reduced for the sake of the physical plant. Documents by DeBernardis (1984), DeCosmo (1978), and the California Postsecondary Education Commission (1983a) underscore the threat of deferred maintenance and reduced equipment expenditures. Somehow, institutional resources will have to be diverted to these problems.

In response to the retrenchment problem, college administrators have an increased emphasis on long-range planning. DeCosmo (1978) argues that in the past, colleges simply added programs to meet emerging needs. Now, he notes, they have to reallocate existing funds. This involves examining institutional goals and objectives, monitoring institutional functioning, and implementing long-range planning. Several ERIC documents and journal articles describe such planning efforts. Keyser and Gonzales (1984) examine how administrators prioritized programs at Linn-Benton Community College on the basis of data on instructional cost per student, demand for the programs, the employment outlook of graduates, the percent of former students who are working and studying in the fields for which they were trained, enrollment retention rates, and the sunk costs of capital investment. Murphy (1983) describes policies related to financial exigency at Harford Community College (Maryland);

these policies require individual program leaders to submit quantitative and qualitative data that can be used by the president in planning and priority setting. Other efforts to plan for fiscal exigencies at Northampton Area Community College (Pennsylvania), Prince George's Community College (Maryland), and Monroe Community College (New York) are described, respectively, by Richardson (1978), Clagett (1981), and Milligan (1982). Fiscal exigencies, in short, have resulted in increased efforts to gather data with which administrators can judge the contributions of individual programs to overall institutional goals. Further information on institutional strategic planning is provided by Myran (1983).

Will long-range planning help colleges maintain quality within limited budgets? This question remains open, because most authors simply describe planning efforts without evaluating their outcomes. Furthermore, institutional quality is rarely defined, and—in any case—some administrators do not believe that the luxury of long-range planning is available in an era of constant change (see Koltai, 1980). Future authors will undoubtedly focus on the effectiveness of institutional planning efforts ushered in by the fiscal exigencies of the 1970s and 1980s.

Differential Salaries for Faculty

Although the question of differential pay rates for faculty has become an important policy issue during the last decade, relatively little literature has been devoted to this subject. The few items available are ably covered by Wagner in Chapter Eleven of this sourcebook. Because of the dearth of literature on this topic, community college administrators are urged to submit institutional documents dealing with differential remuneration to the ERIC database. More information is needed on how administrators go about the task of establishing differential pay scales once the decision has been made to do so.

Additional Information

This sampling of ERIC literature has focused on part-time faculty, retrenchment, and open access. Additional information on these or any other topics related to community college administration or education may be obtained from manual or computer search of ERIC's *Resources in Education* and *Current Index to Journals in Education*.

The full text of the references with an ED number may be obtained from the ERIC Document Reproduction Service (EDRS) in Alexandria, Virginia, or viewed on microfiche at over 730 libraries nationwide. References without an ED number must be obtained through regular library channels. For an EDRS order form and/or a list of libraries in your state that have ERIC microfiche collections, please contact the ERIC Clearinghouse for Junior Colleges, 8118 Math-Sciences Building, UCLA, Los Angeles, California 90024.

References

Anandam, K., Kotler, L., Eisel, E., and Roche, R. A. *RSVP: Feedback Program for Individualized Analysis of Writing. Research Report.* Miami, Fla.: Miami-Dade Junior College, 1979. 99 pp. (ED 191 511)

Beavers, J. L. *A Study of the Correlation Between English Qualifying Exam Scores and Freshman/Developmental English Grades at Wytheville Community College.* Wytheville, Va.: Office of Institutional Research, Wytheville Community College, 1983. 9 pp. (ED 231 487)

Boggs, G. R. "A Response to Uncertainty: The Increased Utilization of Part-Time Instructors in American Community Colleges." *Community/Junior College Quarterly of Research and Practice,* 1984, *8* (1-4), 5-17.

California Postsecondary Education Commission. *Facing the Issue of Facilities Maintenance in California Public Higher Education.* Sacramento: California State Postsecondary Education Commission, 1983a. 34 pp. (ED 232 501)

California Postsecondary Education Commission. *Impact of 1982-83 Budget Constraints On the California Postsecondary Education Commission Survey.* Sacramento: California Postsecondary Education Commission, 1983b. 27 pp. (ED 234 857)

Casey, J. W. *Managing Contraction: An Institution Experiences Contraction. Seattle Community College District, Seattle, Washington, U.S.A.* Seattle, Wash.: Seattle Community College District, 1982. 17 pp. (ED 229 064)

Chausow, H. M., and Barshis, D. *A Developmental Education Program: An Experiment [and] Revised Guidelines for Academic Year 1983 Developmental Education Program.* Chicago: Center for the Improvement of Teaching and Learning, 1983. 10 pp. (ED 231 430)

Clagett, C. A. *Community College Policies for the Coming Financial Squeeze.* Working Paper No. 4. Largo, Md.: Prince George's Community College, 1981. 55 pp. (ED 225 604)

Cohen, A. M. "The Rhetoric of Access." *Change,* 1975, *7* (1), 50-51.

Conkright, A. M. *"Only Connect . . . ": A Passionate Plea for an Integrated Curriculum. An Issue Paper.* Phoenix, Ariz.: Maricopa Community College District, 1982. 26 pp. (ED 231 409)

Cruise, R. J., Furst, L. G., and Klimes, R. E. "A Comparison of Full-Time and Part-Time Instructors at Midwestern Community College." *Community College Review,* 1980, *8* (1), 52-56.

Davis, B., and Luvaas-Briggs, L. *"It's Not My Job"—Basic Skill Development in a Sociology Course, A Shared Solution.* Sacramento: Sacramento City College, 1983. 9 pp. (ED 231 496)

DeBernardis, A. "Excellent Facilities Yield Excellence in Education." *Community and Junior College Journal,* 1984, *54* (5), 35-36.

DeCosmo, R. "Reduced Resources and the Academic Program." In R. L. Alfred (ed.), *Coping With Reduced Resources.* New Directions for Community Colleges, no. 22. San Francisco: Jossey-Bass, 1978.

Donohue, J. P. "Development of Oakton Community College's Graduation/Registration/Advisement System (GRADS) and Standards of Academic Progress (SOAP) Utilizing Computer Resources." Paper presented at the League for Innovation in the Community Colleges and Maricopa Community College Working Conference on Student Information System, Scottsdale, Arizona, February 6-7, 1984. 18 pp. (ED 243 511)

Eliason, N. C. "Part-Time Faculty: A National Perspective." In M. H. Parsons (ed.), *Using Part-Time Faculty Effectively.* New Directions for Community Colleges, no. 30. San Francisco: Jossey-Bass, 1980.

Elioff, I. H. "The Challenge of Faculty Development for Part-Timers in Noncampus Community Colleges." Paper presented at the Conference on Quality in Off-Campus Credit Programs: Challenges, Choices and Concerns, sponsored by the Division of

Continuing Education, Kansas State University, Atlanta, Ga., October 31–November 2, 1983. 19 pp. (ED 243 502)

Forstall, J. C. *Survey of Assessment of Basic Skills in Illinois Public Two-Year Colleges.* Report No. 99. Springfield, Ill.: Lincoln Land Community College, 1984. 8 pp. (ED 248 927)

Friedlander, J. "An ERIC Review: Instructional Practices of Part-Time and Full-Time Faculty." *Community College Review,* 1979, *6* (3), 65–72.

Friedlander, J. *Evaluation of Napa Valley College's Student Orientation, Assessment, Advisement, and Retention Program.* Napa, Calif.: Napa Valley College, 1984. 12 pp. (ED 250 026)

Fryer, T. W., Jr. "Designing New Personnel Policies: The Permanent Part-Time Faculty Member." *Journal of the College and University Personnel Association,* 1977, *28* (2), 14–21.

Guthrie-Morse, B. "The Utilization of Part-Time Faculty." *Community College Frontiers,* 1979, *7* (3), 8–17.

Haase, M. H., and Caffrey, P. *Assessment Procedures, Fall 1982 and Spring 1983. Semi-Annual Research Report, Part I.* Sacramento, Calif.: Sacramento City College, 1983. 89 pp. (ED 231 494)

Haase, M. H., and Caffrey, P. *The Impact of a Coordinated Assessment/Advisement/Placement Process on Student Success and Retention. Statistical Response to a Grant Proposal.* Sacramento, Calif.: Sacramento City College, 1984. 27pp. (ED 243 540)

Hammons, J. O. "Adjunct Faculty: Another Look." *Community College Frontiers,* 1981, *9* (2), 46–53.

Harper, H., Herrig, J., Kelly, J. T., and Schinoff, R. B. *Advisement and Graduation Information System.* Miami, Fla.: Miami–Dade Community College, 1981. 34 pp. (ED 197 776)

Harris, M. E. "Internationalizing Curricula: Articulation Between Two- and Four-Year Colleges and Universities." Paper presented at the annual convention of the International Studies Association, Atlanta, Ga., March 27–31, 1984. 9 pp. (ED 246 941)

Hartman, N. E. *Maximizing the Effectiveness of Reading Tests in the Community College.* St. Louis, Mo.: Saint Louis Community College, 1981. 55 pp. (ED 237 121)

Hector, J. H. *Establishing Cutoff Scores for Placement in Community College Developmental Courses.* Morristown, Tenn.: Walters State Community College, 1984. 20 pp. (ED 246 934)

Henard, K. F., and Adelman, S. I. *A Baker's Dozen Questions about Access: The Unabbreviated Report.* Amarillo, Tex.: Amarillo College, 1982. 16 pp. (ED 226 790)

Henderson, L. N., Jr. *The Status of the Open Door: Florida's Community Colleges in the 1980s.* Gainesville: Institute of Higher Education, University of Florida, 1982. 55 pp. (ED 219 114)

Hyde, W. *A New Look at Community College Access.* Denver, Colo.: Education Commission of the States, 1982. 194 pp. (ED 217 905)

Ireland, J., and Feuers-Jones, A. *The Status and Future of Community Services in the Los Angeles Community College District.* Los Angeles: Los Angeles Community College District, 1980. 30 p. (ED 192 838)

Jones, S. W. "Determining Effective Teaching Behaviors and Staff Development Opportunities for Adjunct Faculty." Ed.D. practicum, Nova University, 1984. 31 pp. (ED 251 131)

Kekke, R. *Who's Mr. Staff: Cheap Labor or Valued Resource?* Cedar Rapids, Iowa: Kirkwood Community College, 1984. 15 pp. (ED 251 134)

Kelly, J. T. and Anandam, K. "Computer-Enhanced Academic Alert and Advisement System." Paper presented at the 1979 CAUSE National Conference, Orlando, Fla., November 27–30, 1979. 39 pp. (ED 216 722)

Keyser, J., and Gonzales, T. *Strategic Planning for Linn-Benton Community College.* Albany, Ore.: Linn-Benton Community College, 1984. 34 pp. (ED 244 679)

Koltai, L. L. *The Agony of Change. Junior College Resource Review.* Los Angeles: ERIC Clearinghouse for Junior Colleges, University of California, 1980. 6 pp. (ED 187 382)

Koltai, L., and Wolf, D. B. "A Reasonable Consensus." *Community and Junior College Journal,* 1984, *55* (1), 42-45.

Landsburg, D., and Witt, S. "Writing Across the Curriculum: One Small Step." Unpublished paper, 1984. 4 pp. (ED 248 922)

Lolley, J. L. "A Comparison of the Use of Instructional Resources by Full-Time and Part-Time Teachers." *Community/Junior College Research Quarterly,* 1980, *5* (1), 47-51.

Losak, J. *Status of Impacts of the Reforms Which Have Been Initiated at Miami-Dade Community College During the Past Five Years.* Research Report no. 83-13. Miami, Fla.: Office of Institutional Research, Miami-Dade Community College, 1983. 10 pp. (ED 237 136)

Losak, J., and Morris, C. *Impact of the Standards of Academic Progress on Student Achievement and Persistence at Miami-Dade Community College.* Research Report No. 83-23. Miami, Fla.: Office of Institutional Research, Miami-Dade Community College, 1983a. 21 pp. (ED 239 698)

Losak, J., and Morris, C. *Projected Impact of Entry and Exit Testing in Secondary and Postsecondary Education.* Research Report No. 83-32. Miami, Fla.: Office of Institutional Research, Miami-Dade Community College, 1983b. 9 pp. (ED 239 677)

Lukenbill, J. D., and McCabe, R. H. *General Education in a Changing Society. General Education Program, Basic Skills Requirements, Standards of Academic Progress at Miami-Dade Community College.* Miami, Fla.: Office of Institutional Research, Miami-Dade Community College, 1978. 98 pp. (ED 158 812)

McCabe, R. H. "Now Is the Time to Reform the American Community College." *Community and Junior College Journal,* 1981, *51* (8), 6-10.

McCabe, R. H. *A Status Report on the Comprehensive Educational Reform of Miami-Dade Community College.* Miami, Fla.: Miami-Dade Community College, 1983. 10 pp. (ED 238 481)

McCright, G. J. "A Study of Perceived Professional Development Needs of Part-Time Faculty Members at Marshalltown Community College." Ed.D. practicum, Nova University, 1983. 37 pp. (ED 242 364)

Marsh, J. P., and Lamb, T. (eds.). *An Introduction to the Part-Time Teaching Situation with Particular Emphasis on Its Impact at Napa Community College.* Napa, Calif.: Napa College, 1975. 46 pp. (ED 125 683)

Matson, J. E. "Reduction and Student Services." In R. L. Alfred (ed.), *Coping with Reduced Resources.* New Directions for Community Colleges, no. 22. San Francisco: Jossey-Bass, 1978.

Miller, C. K. *Success Comparison of High-Risk Students in Two-Year College Transfer Curricula.* Canton, Ohio: Stark Technical College, 1982. 100 pp. (ED 225 624)

Milligan, F. G. *Monroe Community College: A Model Faculty Contractual Agreement: Retraining and Reassignment of Faculty.* Rochester, N.Y.: Monroe Community College, 1982. 32 pp. (ED 216 728)

Mirabeau, R. L. "Administration and the Challenge of Open Enrollment." Paper presented at the National Humanities Conference on Two-Year Colleges, Boston, Mass., November 10-12, 1977. 24 pp. (ED 780 177)

Murphy, M. T. *Policies and Procedures Relating to Program Redirection and Financial Exigency.* Bel Air, Md.: Harford Community College, 1983. 16 pp. (ED 227 910)

Myran, G. A. (ed). *Strategic Management in the Community College.* New Directions for Community Colleges, no. 44. San Francisco: Jossey-Bass, 1983. 129 pp. (ED 238 477)

Neault, L. C. *Phase II. The English Placement Test: A Correlation Analysis.* San Diego, Calif.: San Diego Community College District, 1984. 84 pp. (ED 245 725)

Nichols, D. D., and Stuart, W. H. "In Praise of Fewer Administrators." Unpublished paper. American Association of Community and Junior Colleges, 1983. 26 pp. (ED 227 889)

Parsons, M. H. (ed.). *Using Part-Time Faculty Effectively.* New Directions for Community Colleges, no. 30. San Francisco: Jossey-Bass. 1980. 115 pp. (ED 188 717)

Pedras, M. J. "A Model for the Staff Development of Community College Part-Time Faculty." Paper presented at the International Seminar on Staff, Program, and Organizational Development, Leysin, Switzerland, July 3-8, 1985. 18 pp. (ED 257 514)

Peterson, T. "Part-Time Faculty Compensation and Staff Development in Three Kansas City Area Community Colleges." Graduate seminar paper, University of Missouri, 1982. 24 pp. (ED 225 615)

Phillips, H. "The Care and Feeding of Part-Time Teachers." Paper presented at the national conference of the National Council for Staff, Program, and Organizational Development, Atlanta, Ga., October 27-28, 1984. 8 pp. (ED 251 144)

Pollock, A., and Breuder, R. L. "The Eighties and Part-Time Faculty." *Community College Review,* 1982, *9* (4), 58-62.

Prince George's Community College. *"START": A Computer-Assisted Management Model for Student Testing, Advisement Retention, and Tracking.* Largo, Md.: Department of Human Development, Prince George's Community College, 1983. 68 pp. (ED 235 868)

Ramey, L. *Assessment Procedures for Students Entering Florida Community Colleges: Theory and Practice.* Gainesville: Florida Community Junior College Inter-Institutional Research Council, 1981. 151 pp. (ED 231 474)

Rasor, R. A., and Powell, T. *Predicting English Writing Course Success with the Vocabulary and Usage Subtests of the Descriptive Tests of Language Skills of the College Board.* Sacramento, Calif.: American River College, 1984, 34 pp. (ED 243 535)

Richardson, R. C., Jr. "Adapting to Declining Resources Through Planning and Research." In R. L. Alfred (ed.), *Coping With Reduced Resources.* New Directions for Community Colleges, no. 22. San Francisco: Jossey-Bass, 1978.

Richardson, R. C., Jr. "Future of the Open Door: A Presentation for ACCT." Paper presented at the annual convention of the Association of Community College Trustees, Phoenix, Ariz., October 12-16, 1983a. 8 pp. (ED 235 848)

Richardson, R. C., Jr. "Open Access and Institutional Policy: Time for Re-examination." *Community College Review,* 1983b. *10* (4), 47-51.

Rippey, D. T., and Roueche, J. E. "Implications of Reduced Funding Upon the Open-Door Commitment." *Community College Review,* 1977, *5* (2), 55-58.

Rivera, M. G. "Placement Systems for English Courses in Selected California Community Colleges." Paper presented to the Arizona English Teachers Association and at the Pacific Coast Regional Conference on English in the Two-year College, Phoenix, Ariz., November 6-7, 1981. 14 pp. (ED 235 854)

Roueche, J. E. "Don't Close the Door." *Community and Junior College Journal,* 1981-82, *52* (4), pp. 17, 21-23.

Roueche, J. E., Baker, G. A. III, and Roueche, S. D. "Access With Excellence: Toward Academic Success in College." *Community College Review,* 1985, *12* (4), 4-9.

Rounds, J. C. "Entrance Assessment at Community Colleges: A Decade of Change." Unpublished paper, 1984. 13 pp. (ED 243 552)

Rounds, J. C., and Andersen, D. "Tests in Use in California Community Colleges: Standardized Tests Most Used for Placement in English, Reading, ESL, and Math." Unpublished paper, 1984. 28 pp. (ED 250 037)

Starks, G. "Interdisciplinary Approaches to Retention and Motivation in College." Unpublished paper, 1984. 14 pp. (ED 246 973)

Sussman, H. B. "Institutional Responses to Reduced Resources." In R. L. Alfred (ed.), *Coping With Reduced Resources.* New Directions for Community Colleges, no. 22. San Francisco: Jossey-Bass, 1978.

Turgeon, M. L. "Part-Time Faculty: A Comparative Profile of Characteristics and Effectiveness at Corning Community College." Ed.D. practicum, Nova University, 1983. 55 pp. (ED 244 654)

White, R. A. "Faculty Retraining for Lateral Transfer: An Alternative to Reduction in Force in Community Colleges." Graduate seminar paper, Pepperdine University, 1978. 40 pp. (ED 164 042)

Willett, L. H. "Comparison of Instructional Effectiveness of Full- and Part-Time Faculty." *Community/Junior College Research Quarterly,* 1980, 5 (1), 23-30.

Winter, G., Fadale, L., and Anderson, M. *Faculty Development Manual for Adjunct Staff in Postsecondary Occupational Programs.* Albany: Two-Year College Development Center, State University of New York, 1981. 75 pp. (ED 233 777)

Zoglin, M. L. "Redefining the Role of the Community College in an Era of Declining Resources." *Change,* 1982, *14* (6), 36-38.

Jim Palmer is the assistant director for user services at the ERIC Clearinghouse for Junior Colleges.

Index

A

Abel, E. K., 10, 11, 12
Adelman, S. I., 104, 109
Affirmative action, and part-time faculty, 29
Alfred, R., 82-83, 86
American Association of University Professors (AAUP), 1, 24
Anandam, K., 104, 108, 109
Andersen, D., 104, 111
Anderson, M., 103, 112
Ashby, E., 85, 86
Association of American Colleges, 43-44, 46

B

Baker, G. A., III, 104, 111
Barringer, B. A., 34, 37, 40
Barry, D., 81, 86
Barshis, D., 104, 108
Beavers, J. L., 104, 108
Bender, L. W., 7, 10, 12, 16, 21
Blank, S., 16, 21
Boggs, G. R., 103, 108
Booth, W., 17-18, 22
Bowen, H. R., 62, 63
Bramlett, P., 11, 13
Brawer, F. B., 9, 13, 58, 59, 60, 63
Breneman, D. W., 38, 40
Breuder, R. L., 10, 12, 16, 21, 22, 102, 111
Business and industry, and quality, 60-61

C

Caffrey, P., 104, 109
Caldwell, J., 18, 21, 22
California: part-time faculty in, 26; retrenchment in, 105-106
California Postsecondary Education Commission, 105, 106, 108
Camus, A., 42
Carnegie Council of Policy Studies in Higher Education, 43

Casey, J. W., 106, 108
Chausow, H. M., 104, 108
Chell, C., 16, 19, 22
City College of New York, and open door, 46
Clagett, C. A., 107, 108
Clements, C., 76, 77
Cleveland, H., 83
Cohen, A. M., 9, 13, 58, 59, 60, 63, 105, 108
College Level Academic Skills Test (CLAST), 73, 75
Community colleges: declining status of, 35-36; faculty salaries at, 79-97; information sources for, 101-112; mission of, 34; open door to, 31-53; part-time faculty in, 5-30; realities for, 1-2; retrenchment and quality at, 55-77
Conkright, A. M., 104-105, 108
Cooke, H. L., 11, 13
Corning Community College, and part-time faculty, 103
Cost effectiveness, of part-time faculty, 8-9
Council of Instructional Affairs (Florida), 73
Cross, K. P., 58, 64
Cruise, R. J., 8, 13, 102, 108
Curriculum: planning, and program evaluation, 76-77; as quality focus, 58-59; scope of, and part-time faculty, 9-10

D

Dallas County Community College District, program evaluation in, 75-76, 77
Davis, B., 104, 108
DeBernardis, A., 106, 108
DeCosmo, R., 106, 108
Demaree, W. E., 2, 41-46
Division of Community Colleges (Florida), 73
Donohue, J. P., 104, 108
Dostoevski, F., 42
Dziech, B. W., 1-3

E

Eells, W. C., 7, 9, 13
Eisel, E., 108
Eliason, N. C., 101-102, 108
Elioff, I. H., 103, 108-109
Eliot, T. S., 1
Enarson, H. L., 58, 62, 64
Evaluation. *See* Program evaluation
Evangelauf, J., 2

F

Faculty: part-time, 5-30; salaries for, 79-97
Fadale, L., 103, 112
Feuers-Jones, A., 105, 109
Florida, program evaluation in, 72-73
Forstall, J. C., 104, 109
Friedlander, J., 10, 13, 102, 104, 109
Fryer, T. W., Jr., 102, 109
Furst, L. G., 8, 13, 102, 108

G

Gappa, J. M., 23, 24, 29
G.I. Bill, 34
Gonzales, T., 106, 109
Greenberg, B., 16, 21
Guthrie-Morse, B., 8, 10, 13, 102, 109

H

Haase, M. H., 104, 109
Hammons, J. O., 7, 9, 10, 12, 13, 17, 22, 101, 102, 103, 109
Hansen, L. W., 88-89, 91, 92
Harford Community College, retrenchment at, 106-107
Harper, H., 104, 109
Harris, D. A., 27, 29
Harris, M. E., 105, 109
Hartleb, D. F., 2, 15-22, 23
Hartman, N. E., 104, 109
Hector, J. H., 104 109
Hemingway, E., 2
Henard, K. F., 104, 109
Henderson, L. N., Jr., 103, 109
Herrig, J., 109
Herzberg, F. W., 94, 97
Hurlbut, A. S., 11, 13
Hyde, W., 103, 105, 109

I

Ireland, J., 105, 109

J

Jones, S. W., 103, 109

K

Kafka, F., 42
Katz, D. A., 91, 92
Kekke, R., 103, 109
Kelly, J. T., 104, 109
Keyser, J., 106, 109
Klimes, R., 8, 13, 102, 108
Koltai, L. L., 103, 107, 110
Kotler, L., 108

L

Lamb, T., 102, 110
Landsburg, D., 105, 110
Lane, W. H., 10, 13
Lawrence, B., 62, 64
Leonardo da Vinci, 85
Linn-Benton Community College, retrenchment at, 106
Lolley, J. J., 8, 13, 103, 110
Lombardi, J., 8, 9, 13
Losak, J., 104, 110
Lukenbill, J. D., 104, 110
Luvaas-Briggs, L., 104, 108

M

McCabe, R. H., 33-34, 38-39, 104, 105, 110
McCright, G. R., 103, 110
McGaughey, J. L., 27, 30
McGuire, J. M., 2, 57-64, 71
McQuade, D., 16, 22
Marsh, J. P., 102, 110
Martens, K. J., 58, 64
Matson, J. E., 105, 110
May, W., 84, 86
Mellander, G. A., 2, 47-53
Meyer, T. J., 1, 2
Miami-Dade Community College: program evaluation at, 74-75; reforms at, 33, 38-39, 104
Michelangelo, 85

Middle States Association of Colleges and Schools, 49
Miller, C. K., 104, 110
Miller, E. L., 2, 57-64, 71
Miller, T. M., 36, 40
Milligan, F. G., 107, 110
Mirabeau, R. L., 104, 110
Mission: of community colleges, 34; and quality, 59-60
Monroe Community College, retrenchment at, 107
Morgan, D. A., 59, 64
Morris, C., 104, 110
Munsey, W. R. C., 2, 7-13, 23
Murphy, M. T., 106-107, 110
Myran, G. A., 107, 110

N

Nash, N., 82-83, 86
National Center for Education Statistics, 44
Neault, L. C., 104, 110
Nelson, S. C., 35, 38, 40
New Jersey Department of Higher Education, 49
Nichols, D. D., 106, 110-111
Nigliazzo, M. A., 2, 33-40
Northampton Area Community College, retrenchment at, 107

O

Oakland Community College, retrenchment at, 106
Open door: analysis of, 31-53; background on, 33-34; commitment to, 47-53; conclusions on, 39, 53; criticisms of, 41-43; and declining status, 35-36; fading vision of, 33-40; information sources on, 103-105; as mission, 34; modifications of, 36-37; need for, 45-46; problems from, 48-49; and standards, 49-52; strategies for, 38-39; students served by, 43-46

P

Palmer, J. C., 58, 64, 101-112
Parkersburg Community College, and quality, 60, 61, 62
Parsons, M. H., 27, 30, 103, 111

Part-time faculty: and affirmative action, 29; analysis of, 5-30; approaches to, 26-27; attitudes toward, 17; background on, 15-17, 23-24; benefits of using, 7-13; categories of, 24-25; changes for, 27; conclusions on, 12, 29; cost effectiveness of, 8-9; costs to, 20-21; and curricular scope, 9-10; dependent, 25-26; disadvantages of using, 15-22; and flexibility, 10-11; history of, 7-8; independent, 24-25; information sources for, 101-103; institutional costs of, 17-20; issues for, 23-30; metaphors for, 16-17; and nonclassroom activities, 18-19, 28; percentage of, 7-8, 16; as pool for full-time positions, 11; and public relations, 11-12; recommendations on, 27-29
Passaic County College, reforms at, 48-53
Pedras, M. J., 103, 111
Perkins, J. R., 8, 13
Peterson, T., 103, 111
Phillips, H., 103, 111
Piedmont Virginia Community College, part-time faculty at, 7, 8
Pollock, A., 16, 22, 102, 111
Powell, T., 104, 111
Price, P. H., 10, 13
Prince Georges Community College, 104, 107, 111
Program evaluation: background on, 71-72; campus-level, 73-76; need for, 72; for quality, 71-77; state-level, 72-73
Prokasky, W., 83, 86

Q

Quality: analysis of, 55-77; background on, 57; and business and industry, 60-61; challenge of, 58; commitment to, 57-64; considerations in, 59-63; and curriculum focus, 58-59; and image and reputation, 61; indicators of, 58, 73, 74, 75, 76; information sources on, 105-107; and mission, 59-60; and paring back, 62, 65-69; program evaluation for, 71-77; and program needs, 61-62; and standards, 62-63; summary on, 63, 77

R

Ramey, L., 104, 111
Rasor, R. A., 104, 111
Retrenchment: across-the-board strategy for, 66-67; analysis of, 55-77; background on, 65-66; conclusion on, 69; information sources on, 105-107; selective, 68-69; of weak programs, 65-69
Richardson, R. C., Jr., 58, 64, 104, 105, 107, 111
Rippey, D. T., 105, 111
Ritter, L., 83, 86
Rivera, M. G., 104, 111
Roche, R. A., 108
Rodriguez, R. C., 11, 13
Romanik, D., 73, 77
Rondinone, P. J., 41-42, 46
Roueche, J. E., 104, 105, 111
Roueche, S. D., 104, 111
Rounds, J. C., 104, 111

S

Salaries, differential: administering, 96; analysis of, 79-97; approaches to, 93-97; appropriate action for, 91-92; and attitudes, 83-84, 90; background on, 81-82, 87-88, 93-94; conclusions on, 85-86, 97; and constancy of demand, 82-83, 91; criticisms of, 81-86; factors in, 88-90; forces against, 90-91; information needed on, 107; and money as motivator, 82, 94; need for, 87-92; schedules for, 88, 94-95; and teaching as a trade, 84-85
Schinoff, R. B., 109
Simpson, W. P., 88, 92
Smith, A. B., 2, 71-77
Sojka, G. A., 88, 92
Spoffard, T., 16, 22
Standards: and open door, 49-52; and quality, 62-63
Starks, G., 105, 111
State Board of Community Colleges (Florida), 73
Stewart, P., 58
Stuart, W. H., 106, 110-111
Students, characteristics of, and open door, 43-46
Study Group on the Conditions of Excellence in American Higher Education, 72, 77
Sussman, H. B., 106, 111

T

Tarrant County Community College, and part-time faculty, 103
Temple, R. J., 2, 65-69, 71
Tuckman, B., 16, 22
Tuckman, H. P., 16, 18, 21, 22, 88, 92
Turgeon, M. L., 103, 112

V

Vaughan, G. B., 2, 23-30, 34, 35, 36, 40
Vincent, W. E., 36, 40
Vitler, W., 2, 15-22, 23

W

Wagner, T. E., 2, 87-92, 107
Wattenbarger, J. L., 2, 93-97
White, R. A., 106, 112
Willett, L. H., 8, 13, 102, 112
Winter, G., 103, 112
Witt, S., 105, 110
Wolf, D. B., 103, 110
Woloshin, P. L., 2, 81-86

Y

Yarborough, N. P., 8, 13

Z

Zoglin, M. L., 105, 112